W9-CAV-914

A Stay Against Confusion

Also by Ron Hansen

Hitler's Niece

Atticus

Mariette in Ecstasy

Nebraska

The Assassination of Jesse James by the Coward Robert Ford

Desperadoes

For Children

The Shadowmaker

Editor

You've Got to Read This: Contemporary American Writers Introduce Stories That Held Them in Awe (with Jim Shepard)

You Don't Know What Love Is: Contemporary American Short Stories

A Stay Against Confusion

Essays on Faith and Fiction

Ron Hansen

HarperCollins*Publishers*

HarperCollins books may be purchased for educational, business, or sales promotional use. For information, please write: Special Markets Department, HarperCollins Publishers Inc., 10 East 53rd Street, New York, NY 10022.

FIRST EDITION

Designed by Jackie McKee

Printed on acid-free paper

Library of Congress Cataloging-in-Publication Data

Hansen, Ron.
A stay against confusion : essays on faith and fiction / by Ron Hansen.
p. cm.
Includes bibliographical references.
ISBN 0-06-019666-1
1. Hansen, Ron. 2. Novelist, American—20th century—Biography. 3. Christianity and literature—United States. 4. Christian biography—United States. 5. Fiction—Authorship. I. Title.
PS3558.A5133 Z47 2001

814'.54—dc21 00-056694

00 01 02 03 04 ❖ RRD 10 9 8 7 6 5 4 3 2 1

To My Sisters,

Alice, Laura, and Gini

Contents

Preface: A Stay Against Confusion

The first time I noticed it is lost to me now, but I may have been five or so. At Sunday Mass in Omaha, the priest ascended the stairs to the high pulpit at Holy Angels Church, announced a reading from one of the Gospels, and after a few sentences of the passage I was suddenly aware that the story was familiar to me. Say it was the shockingly concrete scene in Mark where Jesus heals a blind man by wetting the man's eyes with his spit. I found myself anticipating the next moves, certain that the man would say he could see people but they looked like trees walking. And Jesus would lay his hands on the afflicted man's eyes again, and then the man would see everything clearly. The sentences were sure and predictable to me; I felt I was finally their audience; and I realized with a good deal of wonder that the Gospels were like those children's books that my mother or sisters would read to me over and over again. With great seriousness the priest would read aloud the same stunning stories from the life of Christ, and when he was finished reading he would talk intelligently about the meaning of the passage in our own lives, and even the old in the congregation would watch and listen like children being taught.

The liturgical rites were grand theater then, filled with magisterial ceremony, great varieties of mystery and symbol, and a haunting Gregorian chant that sounded good even if poorly sung. And since I could not yet follow the English translation of the priest's Latin in my Missal, I would fix my gaze high overhead on the soft blue sky of the dome on which there was a huge, literal, and beautiful painting of Christ being escorted by the holy angels on his ascension to heaven, his loose white clothing floating off him so that most of his flesh was exposed.

Looking back on my childhood now, I find that churchgoing and religion were in good part the origin of my vocation as a writer, for along with Catholicism's feast for the senses, its ethical concerns, its insistence on seeing God in all things, and the high status it gave to scripture, drama, and art, there was a connotation in Catholicism's liturgies that storytelling mattered. Each Mass was a narrative steeped in meaning and metaphor, helping the faithful to not only remember the past but to make it present here and now, and to bind ourselves into a sharing group so that, ideally, we could continue the public ministry of Jesus in our world.

On the other hand, my vocation as a writer was also called

forth by something unnameable that I can only associate with a yen to live out in my imagination other lives and possibilities, a craving that eventually made acting attractive to my brother Rob and soon made storytelling necessary to me.

In kindergarten, for example, we had an afternoon period of show-and-tell. A few minutes earlier, a boy named Kenneth breathlessly told me about the side altar at some European cathedral his family had visited, where a pressure-sensitive prie-dieu illuminated a crucifix when penitents fell on their knees there to pray. Seeing my fascination, the five-year-old went further, confusing the scene and himself with flashing colors and whirring mechanisms that seemed lifted from a science fiction movie. I fell into my own imagining as Sister Martha went from child to child, asking them to report on adventures, discoveries, encounters, or anything else they thought noteworthy. And then she got to me. And I instinctively said a neighbor had turned a hallway closet into a chapel, with holy pictures everywhere, and there were lots of candles burning all the time, because that was the only light, and there was a kneeler in front of a crucifix and when you knelt on it real blood trickled out of the wounds in Christ's hands and feet. Real blood? Sister Martha asked. Well, it looked like real blood, it was red like blood, and it trickled down his face from the crown of thorns, too. She squinted at me with just a twitch of a smile, and I was shocked, even insulted that she could think I was making this up. Hadn't I seen that hallway closet, that padded kneeler, that crucifix with my own eyes? I could describe the finest detail, I could smell the candle wax as it burned. Stifling her amusement, the kindergarten teacher questioned me more closely, possibly having found a kids-say-the-darndest-things instance that she could present like a chocolate pie to her sisters at dinner, and I just kept embellishing and filling in gaps in the narrative until Sister Martha seemed to decide I was depleted and she shifted to another child. And when I looked at Kenneth, he was wide-eyed and in awe, with no hint of affront for my having stolen his show-and-tell, but with a certain amount of jealousy that I'd seen a prie-dieu that was so far superior to his and, worse, seemed to have tried to selfishly keep it to myself.

Within the year I would be reading on my own and finding out about children's books and children's authors and their need to do just what I did: to alter facts that seemed imposed and arbitrary, to intensify scenes and situations with additions and falsifications, and to ameliorate the dull and slack commodities of experience with the zest of the wildest imaginings.

The first author whose name I remembered and whose stories I hunted down was Jules Verne, whom I avidly read in third grade. In fourth it was Albert Payson Terhune—I even named our foundling pup "Lad"—and *Peck's Bad Boy* by George Wilbur Peck, with its gladdening irony that a child who was continually getting into trouble with grownups might simply be just acting like children do. Then it was fifth grade and the Hardy Boys and Tom Swift, books meant for kids my age but which seemed hopelessly old-fashioned and did not thrill me nearly so much as the tales of Edgar Allan Poe, who so hooked me that I held his book of horror stories open in my lap to sneak peeks at as I pretended to take classroom notes. I was drawing and painting then, not writing fiction. A friend's father was an illustrator and I fantasized that I would have a job like that when I got out of school. But gradually an urgency to write fiction took over; it was a vocation that seemed so exalted and sacred and beyond me I would not even talk about it.

In "Confessions of a Reluctant Catholic," Alice McDermott recalls learning to be a writer, which "seemed to me from the outset to be an impossible pursuit, one for which I had no preparation or training, or even motive, except for a secret and undeniable urge to do so." She'd discovered that "fiction made the chaos bearable, fiction transformed the absurdity of our brief lives by giving context and purpose and significance to every gesture, every desire, every detail. Fiction transformed the meaningless, fleeting stuff of daily life into the necessary components of an enduring work of art."

The intuition of the fiction writer is similar to that of the scientist, that the world is governed by rules and patterns that are, by analysis and experiment, detectable, that the hidden mysteries of nature can be interrogated and solved. I have run into people who don't read fiction because they feel it's founded on fabrications and swindles and worthless extenuations of reality—a famous professional golfer once complained about English classes in college where he was forced to read "these big, fat books that weren't even true"—but for many of us fiction holds up to the light, fathoms, simplifies, and refines those existential truths that, without such interpretation, seem all too secret, partial, and elusive. And that, of course, is the goal of religion as well.

Many writers are agnostic and have as their religion art, but just as many are conscious that the source of their gifts is God and have found thanksgiving, worship, and praise of the Holy Being to be central to their lives and artistic practice. In *An American Requiem: God, My Father, and The War That Came Between Us,* James Carroll wrote that, "The very act of story-telling, of arranging memory and invention according to the structure of narrative is, by definition, holy." And in a later interview Carroll stated that "my notion of narrative informs my faith, and my notion of faith informs my idea of what writing is for."

Writing not only gives form and meaning to our sometimes disorderly existence, but gives the author the chance for self-disclosure and communion with others, while giving readers a privileged share in another's inner life that, perhaps imperceptibly, questions and illuminates their own. Reading attentively, connecting our lives with those of fictional characters, choosing ethically and emotionally just as they do or in contradistinction to them, we enter the realm of the spirit where we simultaneously discover our likeness to others and our difference, our uniqueness. Questioning ourselves and our world, finding in it, for all its coincidence, accidents, and contingencies a mysterious coherence, we may become aware of a horizon beyond which abides the One who is the creator and context of our existence.

In the preface to his *Collected Poems*, Robert Frost wrote that a poem "begins in delight and ends in wisdom, it inclines to the impulse, it assumes direction with the first line laid down, it runs a course of lucky events, and ends in a clarification of life—not necessarily a great clarification, such as sects and cults are founded on, but in a momentary stay against confusion."

Clarification of life is not only what we have always sought in our reading and our religions, but is as well the primary motive for my writing the fourteen essays on faith and fiction included here.

A Stay Against Confusion

Writing as Sacrament

In 1993, Gregory Wolfe, the publisher and editor of Image: A Journal of the Arts & Religion, *invited me to speak at a conference in New Harmony, Indiana, that the journal was sponsoring. Ironically, though the conference would be addressing the concerns of writers and artists whose visions were shaped by religious belief, its theme of "Silence, Cunning, and Exile: Saying the Unsayable in the '90s" was taken from James Joyce's autobiographical novel* A Portrait of the Artist as a Young Man *and Stephen Dedalus's renunciation of his Catholic faith in favor of service to the god of Art. Speaking to his friend Cranly near the end of the novel, Stephen Dedalus says:*

> You have asked me what I would do and what I would not do. I will tell you what I will do and what I will not do. I will not serve that in which I no longer believe whether it call itself my home, my fatherland, or my church: and I will try to express myself in some mode of life or art as freely as I can and as wholly as I can, using for my defence the only arms I allow myself to use—silence, exile, and cunning.

The rebellion against nation, culture, and religion that seemed singular in the first years of the twentieth century would be taken up on a grand scale by others as modernism and postmodernism found predominance in the arts. And so the situation is now, to some, reversed: that in a society that seems increasingly secular and post-biblical it is now writers and artists of faith who may feel exiled or silenced, who may feel they can say the unsayable only through cunning. "Writing as Sacrament" records my own experiences of approaching the mystery of faith in my fiction.

Writing as Sacrament

When Saint Jerome translated the Bible into the Latin Vulgate, he chose the Latin *sacramentum*, sacrament, for the Greek *mysterion*, mystery. We understand those words to be quite different, but their difference is an efficient way of getting at my argument that good writing can be a religious act.

In the synoptic Gospels *mysterion* generally referred to the secrets of the kingdom of heaven, and, in Saint Paul's Epistles, to Christ himself as the perfect revelation of God's will. Tertullian introduced the term *sacramentum* as we know it when he talked about the rite of Christian initiation, understanding the word to mean a sacred action, object, or means. And Saint Augustine further clarified the term by defining sacraments as "signs pertaining to things divine, or visible forms of an invisible grace."

Eventually more and more events were seen as sacraments until the sixteenth century, when the Protestant Reformation confined the term to baptism and eucharist, the two Gospel sacraments, and the Roman Catholic Council of Trent decreed that signs become sacraments only if they become channels for grace. Twentieth-century theology has used the term in a far more inclusive way, however. *The Oxford Companion to the Bible* describes sacraments "as occasions of encounter between God and the believer, where the reality of God's gracious actions needs to be accepted in faith."

Writing, then, can be viewed as a sacrament insofar as it provides graced occasions of encounter between humanity and God. As Flannery O'Connor noted in *Mystery and Manners*, "the real novelist, the one with an instinct for what he is about, knows that he cannot approach the infinite directly, that he must penetrate the natural human world as it is. The more sacramental his theology, the more encouragement he will get from it to do just that."

Even secular interpretations point to the fiction writer's duty to express the Mystery at the heart of metaphysics. In the famous preface to his novel *The Nigger of the "Narcissus,"* Joseph Conrad defined a fictional work of art as

> a single-minded attempt to render the highest kind of justice to the visible universe, by bringing to light the truth, manifold and one, underlying its every aspect. It is an attempt to find in its forms, in its colours, in its light, in its shadows, in the aspects of matter, and in the facts of life what of each is

> fundamental, what is enduring and essential—their one illuminating and convincing quality—the very truth of their existence.

The highest kind of justice to the visible universe often leads to the highest kind of humility about ourselves. Writing about craft in *The Art of Fiction*, John Gardner held that "the value of great fiction . . . is not just that it entertains us or distracts us from our troubles, not just that it broadens our knowledge of people and places, but also that it helps us to know what we believe, reinforces those qualities that are noblest in us, leads us to feel uneasy about our faults and limitations."

Writers seeking to express a religious vision often help their readers by simply providing, as Gardner put it,

> trustworthy but inexpressible models. We ingest metaphors of good, wordlessly learning to behave more like Levin than like Anna (in *Anna Karenina*), more like the transformed Emma (in Jane Austen's novel) than like the Emma we first meet in the book. This subtle, for the most part wordless knowledge is the "truth" great fiction seeks out.

But I have identified in my own experience and that of many other Christian and Jewish writers that there comes a time when we find the need and the confidence to face the great issues of God and faith and right conduct more directly.

My first published book was *Desperadoes*, a historical novel about the Dalton gang from their hardscrabble beginnings, through their horse-rustling and outlawry in Oklahoma, to the fatal day in 1892 when all but one of the gang were killed in bank robberies in their hometown of Coffeyville, Kansas. "Crime does not pay" is a biblical theme, as is the book's focus on honor, loyalty, integrity, selfishness, and reckless ambition—the highest calling Bob Dalton seems to have felt was to be as important as Jesse James. But my own religious experience does not figure greatly in *Desperadoes*; most people read the book as a highfalutin Western, a boys-will-be-boys adventure full of hijinks and humor and bloodshed.

I fell into my second book because of the first. *The Assassination of Jesse James by the Coward Robert Ford* is another historical novel, but is far darker than *Desperadoes* because I was far more insistent on a Christian perspective on sin and redemption and forgiveness. These were bad guys I was writing about, guys who were sons of preachers but did the wrong thing so blithely and persistently it was like they'd got their instructions all bollixed up. If Jesse James was a false messiah for those Southerners still in civil war with the finance companies and the railroads, then Bob Ford was both his Judas and his Barabbas, a self-important quisling who hoped to be famous and who got off scot-free for the killing of his famous friend, but who was hounded out of more than one town afterward until he ended up as a saloonkeeper in Creede, Colorado. There he himself was killed at the hands of a man who claimed he was evening the score.

It's a form of bad sportsmanship for fiction writers to complain that too few reviewers pick up their subtexts, but in fact I was disappointed that the general reading of the book on Jesse James was pretty much as it was for *Desperadoes*. Hidden beneath the praise were the questions: Why is this guy writing *Westerns*? When oh when is he going to give his talent to a subject that matters?

In his essay "Tradition and the Individual Talent," T. S. Eliot asserted that great writing requires a perpetual surrender of the writer as he or she is in the present in order to pay homage and service to a tradition of literature in the past. "The progress of an artist," he wrote, "is continual self-sacrifice, a continual extinction of personality." I was following Eliot's precepts in the wholesale subtraction of my own personality and the submersion of my familial and religious experiences in my retelling of history in my first two novels, and yet I was frustrated that my fiction did not more fully communicate a belief in Jesus as Lord that was so important, indeed central, to my life.

The English novelist and critic G. K. Chesterton wrote in his conclusion to *Heretics*: "A [writer] cannot be wise enough to be a great artist without being wise enough to be a philosopher. A [writer] cannot have the energy to produce good art without having the energy to wish to pass beyond it. A small artist is content with art; a great artist is content with nothing except everything." Everything for me, and for Chesterton, was the mystery of the Holy Being as it was, and is, incarnated in human life.

Everything for me, to go even further, was the feeling that Christianity is difficult, but that Christianity is worth it. I finally got around to a fuller expression of that in my third novel.

Mariette in Ecstasy concerns a seventeen-year-old woman, Mariette Baptiste, who joins the Convent of Our Lady of Sorrows in upstate New York as a postulant in 1906. Her older sister, Annie, or Mother Céline, is the prioress there and on Christmas Eve, 1906, Mother Céline dies of cancer and is buried. On the next day, Christmas, Mariette is given the stigmata—those wounds in the hands, feet, and side resembling those that Christ suffered on the cross. Whether Mariette is a sexual hysteric full of religious wishful thinking or whether her physical wounds are indeed supernaturally caused is the subject of the novel.

I first thought about writing *Mariette in Ecstasy* after finishing Saint Thérèse de Lisieux's *Story of a Soul.* She was the third of her sisters to enter the Carmelite convent of Lisieux where her oldest sister was prioress and, like Mariette, she soon became a favorite there. You may know that Thérèse was just fifteen at the time she entered religious life and she did so little that was outwardly wonderful during her nine years as a nun that when she died of tuberculosis at twenty-four one of the sisters in the convent with her feared there would be nothing to say about Thérèse at the funeral. She did perform the ordinary duties of religious life extraordinarily well, emphasizing simplicity, obedience, and self-forgetfulness over the harsh physical mortifications that were common in France at that time, and she impressed some with her childlike faith in God the Father and with her passionate love of Jesus. She *can* seem sentimental at times, and there are psychologists who'd diagnose Thérèse as neurotic, but then there are people like me who have a profound respect and awe for her in spite of her perceived excessiveness. When you have a tension like that you're halfway to having a plot.

About then, too, I happened upon *Lettres Portugaises*, a collection of letters falsely presumed to have been written by Sister Mariana Alcoforado about her frantic love affair with a French courtier in the eighteenth century. At one point she supposedly wrote the Chevalier de C—: "I thank you from the bottom of my heart for the desperation you cause me, and I detest the tranquility in which I lived before I knew you."

I was stunned and excited by that line. Emotions like that, I knew, would be at the heart of the novel. I hatched a tale influenced by both those books in which I pretended that the nun I'd modeled on Saint Thérèse de Lisieux would have a kind of love affair with Jesus, with all of a romance's grand exaltations and disappointments, and its physical manifestation would be Christ's wounds from the crucifixion. Further reading about religious women and the phenomenon of the stigmata acquainted me with Anne Catherine Emmerich, Louise Lateau, Theresa Neumann, and, in particular, Gemma Galgani—all of them stigmatics in the late nineteenth and early twentieth centuries.

Some parts of the letters that Mariette writes in the novel are paraphrased from confessions written by Saint Gemma Galgani in 1900 and included in a hard-to-find book called *Letters and Ecstasies.* Quotidian life in my fictional religious order, the Sisters of the Crucifixion, is based on Thomas Merton's account of Cistercian life in *The Waters of Siloe.* The mass hysteria hinted at in my book was a product of my looking into Aldous Huxley's fascinating history, *The Devils of Loudun.* Simple scenes of the sisters at work and recreation were inspired by a book of photographs taken at the Carmelite convent in Lisieux by Thérèse's sister Céline. The first investigation of Mariette's stigmata is taken from the medical diagnosis of Padre Pio's stigmata in the 1920s. Cribbing and stealing from hundreds of sources, I finally allowed my factual sources to be distorted and transmuted by figurative language, forgetfulness, or by the personalities of the fictional characters.

I hoped to present in Mariette's life a faith that gives an intellectual assent to Catholic orthodoxy, but doesn't forget that the origin of religious feeling is the graced revelation of the Holy Being to us in nature, in the flesh, and in all our faculties. If I may be permitted the immodesty of quoting a review, I was trying to stake claim, as Pico Iyer put it, to "a world as close and equivocal as Emily Dickinson's, alive with the age-old American concerns of community and wildness, of sexual and spiritual immensities, of transcendence and its discontents."

Saying the unsayable it possibly was—I felt free to try it because I knew the book would get published somewhere, even if it were a small press, and I knew the books I liked best were not those that seemed tailored to contemporary tastes but those that were unfashionable, refractory, insubordinate, that seem the products not of a market analysis but of a writer's private obsession.

But in my rebellion against what Yale law professor Stephen L. Carter has termed "the culture of disbelief," I did not feel obligated, as Catholic fiction writers in the forties and fifties often did, to be conformist, high-minded, and pure, as if I were seeking a *nihil obstat* from the chancery. As Robert Stone pointed out in "The Reason for Stories," his essay on moral fiction:

> It must be emphasized that the moral imperative of fiction provides no excuse for smug moralizing, religiosity, or propaganda. On the contrary, it forbids them. Nor does it require that every writer equip his work with some edifying message advertising progress, brotherhood, and light. It does not require a writer to be a good man, only a good wizard.

In fact there may be no obligation for a Christian writer or artist to overtly treat Christian themes. Writing about "Catholic Novelists and Their Readers," Flannery O'Connor affirmed fiction writers whose only objective was being "hotly in pursuit of the real." She elaborates by noting that

> St. Thomas Aquinas says that art does not require rectitude of the appetite, that it is wholly concerned with the good of that which is made. He says that a work of art is good in itself, and this is a truth that the modern world has largely

> forgotten. We are not content to stay within our limitations and make something that is simply a good in and by itself. Now we want to make something that will have some utilitarian value. Yet what is good in itself glorifies God because it reflects God. The artist has his hands full and does his duty if he attends to his art. He can safely leave evangelizing to the evangelists.

Evangelization for Jesus was generally by means of parables that were often so bewilderingly allusive that his disciples would ask for further explanations of his meaning. Mark has it that "he did not speak to [the crowds] without a parable, but privately to his own disciples he explained everything." (Mk 4:33–34.) Christ's parables are metaphors that do not contract into simple denotation but broaden continually to take on fresh nuances and connotations. Parables invite the hearer's interest with familiar settings and situations but finally veer off into the unfamiliar, shattering their homey realism and insisting on further reflection and inquiry. We have the uneasy feeling that *we* are being interpreted even as we interpret them. Early, pre-Gospel versions seem to have resembled Zen koans in which hearers are left hanging until they find illumination through profound meditation. A kind of koan occurs in the Gospel of Luke when Jesus compares the kingdom of God to "leaven which a woman took and hid in three measures of flour, till it was all leavened." (Lk 13:21.)

We are challenged, in Jesus' parables, to figure out how we

are like wheat sown in a field, or lost sheep, or mustard seed, or the evil tenants of a householder's vineyard, and in the hard exercise of interpretation we imitate and make present again the graced interaction between the human and the divine.

My fourth novel, *Atticus*, was a retelling of what's often called the parable of the prodigal son, though it's the father who's most truly excessive, having far more love and forgiveness than his son feels he deserves. Without giving away too much of the plot of what is, after all, a mystery, I can offer this: *Atticus* is the story of a Colorado rancher named Atticus Cody who, when he hears that his wild and wayward son Scott has committed suicide, journeys to a town full of expatriated Americans on the Mexican Caribbean in order to recover the body. While there, Atticus happens upon enough factual oversights and inconsistencies to infer that his son was murdered, and he tries to find out who the murderer is.

Mariette in Ecstasy is a parable of a young woman's quest for God; *Atticus* is a parable of God's continuing quest for an intimate relationship with us. Each focuses on seekers, for religion and fiction have in common the unquenchable yearning to achieve the impossible, fathom the unfathomable, hold on to what is fleeting and evanescent and seen, in Saint Paul's words, "as through a glass, darkly." (1 Cor 13:12.)

I hesitate to say more for fiction is far better experienced than interpreted. And so it is with sacraments. To fully understand a symbol is to kill it. So the Holy Being continually finds new ways to proclaim itself to us, first and best of all in the symbols of Christ's life, then in Scripture, and finally in created things, whether they be the glories of nature or art or other human beings. And those symbols will not be objects but actions. As theologian Nathan Mitchell puts it, "Symbols are not things people invent and interpret, but realities that 'make' and interpret a people. . . . Symbols are places to live, breathing spaces that help us discover what possibilities life offers."

The job of fiction writers is to fashion those symbols and give their readers the feeling that life has great significance, that something is going on here that matters. Writing will be a sacrament when it offers in its own way the formula for happiness of Pierre Teilhard de Chardin. Which is: First, be. Second, love. Finally, worship. We may find it's possible that if we do just one of those things completely we may have done all three.

Faith and Fiction

In "Religion and Literature" John Updike noted that the English Victorians generally wrote with the presumption of a religious sensibility on the part of their readers, but that the modernists, responding to the wreckage of conviction wrought by Darwin, Freud, and Marx, sought to make art itself their religion. And so the twentieth century became, for many, an age of disbelief. "Yet it remains curiously true," Updike wrote, "that the literary artist, to achieve full effectiveness, must assume a religious state of mind—a state that looks beyond worldly standards of success and failure. A mood of exaltation should possess the language, a vatic tension and rapture. Even a grimly tragic view, like that of King Lear, *Samuel Beckett, Céline, and Herman Melville, must be expounded with a certain rapt celebrative air. The work of literary art springs from the world and adheres to it but is distinctly different in substance. We enter it, as readers, expecting an intensity and shapeliness absent in our lives. A realm above nature is posed—a supernatural, in short. Aesthetic pleasure, like religious ecstasy, is a matter of inwardness, elevation, and escape."*

In the fall of 1996 I was asked to give the Bannan Lecture at Santa Clara University by Denise Carmody, who chaired the Religious Studies Department. She proposed as my topic "Faith and Fiction." Mr. Updike's essay was unavailable to me then, but I think of it as fraternal to some of the thoughts expressed below.

FAITH AND FICTION

Kindergarten. Omaha. 1952. After morning recess, our Dominican teacher, Sister Martha, assembled the kindergartners in our dank basement classroom in Holy Angels Grade School and told us we'd be putting on a Christmas pageant for our parents. She then scanned our faces while reading from a sheet of paper that named whom we'd portray. Cynthia Bash, the prettiest girl, got to play Mary, and John Kocarnik, the tallest boy, got to play Joseph, choices I probably would have made if asked. But then three boys I found, at best, annoying were assigned the roles of Magi, whom I knew got to wear the fanciest costumes, and a handful of girls were joined into choirs of angels, and finally my twin brother, Rob, and some troublemakers and oafs were handed the no-line jobs of shepherds. And that was it. My name had not been mentioned. Of all the kindergartners at Holy Angels Grade School—and there were plenty in that age of baby boom—I was the only one without a role in the Christmas play. I felt ashamed that I'd offended God in such a way that he was forbidding me a part. And I was afraid that I'd flunked kindergarten as I'd seen some whiny and incontinent children do. Wanting to know for sure just how bad my situation was, I got the gumption to walk up to Sister Martha at playtime and while fighting off tears told her she'd left me out. To my astonishment, she was not irritated at me. She seemed, instead, embarrassed that she'd given a role to one of the Hansen twins and not the other. She probably had intended to be the one to recite the story of the nativity from the Gospel according to Luke, but on seeing my worried face she was inspired by pity to say, "Well, we'll need a narrator. You can be Saint Luke."

The last shall be first indeed. Classmates looked at me with jealousy when I confided to them about it, and even my folks seemed impressed and surprised that Sister had honored me with such a hallowed role. My kindergarten friends were each given little scraps of paper on which their lines had been printed out in order to practice them aloud with an older child or parent, but I handed over to my mother a full page of an Indian-head tablet that was filled with handwriting I couldn't yet read.

We'd sit at the dining room table at night and she'd read a sentence from chapter two of Luke until I could repeat it, and then she'd go on to another sentence. I have a sense of the great language acquisition gifts of children when I recall how little we actually practiced those lines before I had them fast in my head. Meanwhile my father was proudly predicting that I'd perhaps be a great public speaker or politician one day. Dwight Eisenhower had just been elected president and one of his speeches was featured on television. My father pointed to Ike and said, "Maybe that'll be Ronnie when he grows up." All I could think of was that he meant I'd someday be horribly dull and bald.

On the night of the Christmas pageant, as a hundred people found their seats on folding chairs, I stood off to the side in a turban made from one of my sister's pink towels and in my own striped bathrobe from home, but unfortunately without the filthy charcoal mustache and beard that my friends who were shepherds wore, so my pleasure was incomplete. While the kindergarten girls sang "O Little Star of Bethlehem," I saw my folks grinning hopefully at their twin sons while my eleven-year-old sister Gini frowned at me in her *Don't screw this up, I have friends here* way. And then with the song finished, and Sister nodding me forward, I walked to the front of the audience and in the high scream of a four-year-old projecting his voice, I announced, "At that time, there went forth a decree from Caesar Augustus that a census of the whole world should be taken!" On and on I went, reciting sentences I didn't fully understand. "And it came to pass while they were there, that the days for her to be delivered were fulfilled. And she brought forth her firstborn Son, and wrapped Him in swaddling clothes, and laid Him in a manger, because there was no room for them in the inn." When I finished I felt Sister Martha's sigh of relief that I hadn't forgotten anything, and I watched as my friends completed their histrionic pantomime of stargazing, childbirth, and adoration. The Magi sang, "We Three Kings" and we all joined together on "Hark the Herald Angels

Sing," and then it was over and the families applauded their own.

I frequently have been asked when it was that I first had the impulse to be a fiction writer, and I find myself often thinking of that kindergarten play and of those hundred grown-ups and older children whom I knew weren't listening to me but to those fascinating and archaic words, "betrothed," "swaddling," "manger." I felt the power that majestic language had for an audience, that they'd been held rapt not just because of what Luke and I reported but because of the way we said it.

Luke is the most writerly of the Evangelists. Embellishing, adapting, and harmonizing, he does what fiction writers do to hook and hold his audience and get his message across. Even his impatience with other accounts of Christ's life is the sign of a genius whose own faith has found too little affirmation in the accounts of varying worth being offered at the time, for the first paragraph of Luke's Gospel makes it clear that it is a fusion of faith and historical narrative handed down to him by the followers of Jesus and those fervent heralds of the good news whom he calls "ministers of the word." Luke saw it as his vocation to be one of them, to examine what was being said, to "follow all things closely," and to put order and the hard eye of probability on what was possibly for him a frustrating hodgepodge of reminiscences, miracle stories, sayings of Jesus, a passion narrative, and theological interpretations, as well as hearsay, misunderstandings, and heretical fabrications.

A high order of craft and planning and mastery of the

storyteller's art is plainly evident throughout all the Gospels, and yet though they are, like fictions, things made or formed (the Latin *fictio* means shaped or feigned), they have their foundation in a Christ whom their authors were willing to die for. Yet one need not have faith in Christ to be influenced by his story, for we have seen many nineteenth-and twentieth-century novels with no religious pretensions whatsoever whose trajectories imitate that of the life of Jesus of Nazareth.

We generally find in them an initiating incident or graced event that incites the protagonist to a quest for a higher goal. With the rising action of the plot, he or she often gathers friends who share in the quest, and ever greater successes are achieved, obstacles are overcome, enemies are sundered, until a final triumph seems assured. But there is a forbidding crisis in which the protagonist is offered the choice to go ahead in spite of the dangers, or to follow another path, and in that high noon of the soul, the protagonist faces the future abandoned and alone. And then, when all seems lost, by dint of the hero's force of will, a greater victory than seemed attainable is finally won.

Christ's story is so primary to our literature that the eyes of faith can find it in a thousand variations. Look at William Faulkner's *A Fable*, Harper Lee's *To Kill a Mockingbird*, John Irving's *A Prayer for Owen Meany,* and Tom Wolfe's *The Electric Kool-Aid Acid Test*; or, in film, *Mr. Smith Goes to Washington, Cool Hand Luke,* and *Shane.*

We look to fiction for self-understanding, for analogies of

encounter, discovery, and decision that will help us contemplate and change our lives. And so it was for Jesus himself as he formulated his parables. Each of them is Christ's symbolic way of telling us what has been revealed to him in prayer about the Mystery we call God, about Christ's ministry in the world, and of the Father's will for us all.

When we chance upon a metaphor or simile in our reading, we may not notice that we are first halted by the obvious falsity of the statement—the heavyweight boxer Muhammad Ali did not truly "float like a butterfly, sting like a bee"—and then are forced to find connections and similarities we may not have noticed. And because there is no real equivalence, no meshing of objects, our interpretation is never finished, only abandoned. And so it is with parables.

Whenever necessary throughout the Gospels, Jesus offers the faithful proverbs and ways of praying and rules of right conduct and signs of his healing power. But his favorite method of teaching seems to have been in parables because stories so well fuse the feelings of immanence and transcendence that are the two primary qualities of religious experience.

Often in Christ's familiar and very concrete parables there is an upsetting element—a harvest like no other, or homicides in a vineyard—that skews quotidian reality to such an extent that we are obliged to undertake a new way of thinking, to find in our paltry circumstances occasions for surprise, revelation, and self-transcendence.

Even at his last supper, in the Gospel of John, Jesus teaches his friends wholly through metaphors and cryptic turns of phrase. Everything is obliquely stated; it is theology through conundrum. We can practically feel his disciples squirming in uneasiness and wonder. "Where I am going, you cannot follow me now; but you will follow me afterward." "I am the true vine, and my Father is the vinegrower. He removes every branch in me that bears no fruit. Every branch that bears fruit he prunes to make it bear more fruit." "A little while, and you will no longer see me, and again a little while, and you will see me." And finally, "I have said these things in figures of speech. The hour is coming when I will no longer speak to you in figures, but will tell you plainly of the Father."

Jesus was, in Max Weber's terminology, both an ethical prophet—one who outlines rules of conduct for his followers—and an exemplary prophet—one who presents his own life as an example to his followers. And he is never so exemplary as in his Passion. The hour comes when Christ says he will tell us plainly of the Father, but instead he offers us the mysteries of his crucifixion and resurrection. We are told plainly that he cannot hit the nail on the head, that the Word is inexpressible, that it is a burgeoning, a florescence, an opening out into further interpretation. Were the Gospels more biographical, our thinking about Christ would have been more confined, conservative, and hopelessly bound up in human predilections and prejudices.

We instead have a kind of myth, a history full of facts and truths but also a fiction formed with harmony, proportion, and beauty, and fully at ease with uncertainties, metaphor, and poetic fancy.

We have a tendency to separate heaven and earth, soul and body, mind and matter, the unseen and the seen. Myth unites them. Myth honors our intuitions, frees our imaginations, mediates between those things we can explain and those things we cannot explain but in our heart of hearts *know*. We fall in love unreasonably. We act on premonitions, inklings, and perplexing needs. Who among us have held time in our hands? And yet we know we are changed by it. Our lives are filled with mysteries and miracles, coincidence, hunches, and revelations, feelings that have no basis in anything we can put a finger on. Myth pays homage to those intangibles, acknowledging that they are as fully a part of our experience as the tulip glass of Veuve Clicquot we had the other night.

In the ninth of his "Eleven Addresses to the Lord," the poet John Berryman says of the Holy Being, "an old theologian / asserts that even to say You exist is misleading." Our fragile human language, attenuated by imprecision, overuse, and false associations is not up to the hard task of talking about the infinite. Anthony DeMello has even adduced that any image we have of God is more *unlike* him than like him. We seem to be far better off if we try to determine who the Creator is by considering creation, by finding parables of holiness and grace in the world around us.

Saint Ignatius of Loyola was doing just that when, in his "Contemplation to Attain the Love of God" in the *Spiritual Exercises*, he urged retreatants to consider "how God dwells in creatures: in the elements giving them existence, in the plants giving them life, in the animals conferring upon them sensation, in man bestowing understanding. So He dwells in me and gives me being, life, sensation, intelligence; and makes a temple of me, since I am created in the likeness and image of the Divine Majesty."

In finding God in all things, Saint Ignatius was possibly inspired by the postresurrection appearances of Christ to his friends in which they so often mistook who he was: a gardener near the sepulcher, a vagabond on the road to Emmaus, a lone figure on the shore of the Sea of Tiberias offering the fishermen free advice about where they should cast their nets. Christ seemed to be teaching his friends that he will be with them always, as he promised, but in the world at large and in the faces of strangers.

A faith-inspired fiction has a fondness for humanity and finds cause for celebration in the beauties of the natural world. A faith-inspired fiction is ever aware that we are on holy ground. And at the same time that fiction shares in the communion expressed in the famous lines of Reverend John Donne, that "any man's death diminishes *me*, because I am involved in *Mankinde*; /And therefore never send to know for whom the bell tolls; It tolls for *thee*."

In the finest of our fictions, whether it be Willa Cather's *Death Comes for the Archbishop* or Walker Percy's *The Moviegoer*, we have a sense of humanity functioning as it generally does, but at a higher and inspired level where harmonies are revealed, order is discovered, the questions that lie hidden in our hearts are given their just due. We think, if we are Christians, that this is what it is to live fully in the presence of grace. We glimpse, if only through a glass darkly, the present and still-to-come kingdom of God.

And it seems to me we have it as an obligation to witness to what God has revealed, holding to the testimony of Psalm 40, where it is written:

> I have told the glad news of deliverance in the great
> congregation; see, I have not restrained my lips, as you
> know, O LORD.
> I have not hidden your saving help within my heart,
> I have spoken of your faithfulness and your salvation;
> I have not concealed your steadfast love and your faithfulness from the great congregation.
>
> (Ps 40:9–10)

Writing stories is a good way of doing that, but how to avoid homiletics, the shoehorning in of religious belief, the sabotage of the fictional dream by forcing one's characters to perform the role of mouthpieces? So-called Christian fiction is often in fact pallid allegory, or a form of sermonizing, or is a reduction into formula, providing first-century, Pauline solutions to oversimplified problems, sometimes yielding to a Manichean dualism wherein good and evil are plainly at war, or offering as Christianity conservative politics. We cannot call a fiction Christian just because there is no irreligion in it, no skepticism, nothing to cause offense, for such a fiction, in its evasions, may have also evaded, in Karl Rahner's words, "that blessed peril that consists in encountering God."

A faith-inspired fiction squarely faces the imponderables of life, and in the fiction writer's radical self-confrontation may even confess to desolation and doubt. Such fiction is instinctive rather than conformist, intuitive rather than calculated; it features vital characters rather than comforting types, offers freedom and anomaly rather than foregone conclusions, invites thoughtfulness not through rational argument, but through asking the right questions. A faith-inspired fiction is, as Anthony DeMello has said of story, the shortest distance between human understanding and truth.

While it may be hard to believe now, in the late nineteenth century Cardinal John Henry Newman was forced to defend having literature courses at all in a Catholic university. His argument was "if Literature is to be made a study of human nature, you cannot have a Christian Literature. It is a contradiction in terms to attempt a sinless Literature of sinful man. You may gather together something very great and high, something higher than Literature ever was; and when you have done so, you will find that it is not Literature at all."

Writing with faith is a form of praying. Evelyn Waugh maintained prayer ought to consist of adoration, contrition, thanksgiving, and supplication. And so it is in the writing of fiction, in which authors can adore God through their alertness to creation and to the Spirit that dwells in their talent; confess their own faults by faithfully recording the sins, failings, and tendencies of their characters; offer thanksgiving through the beauty of form, language, and thought in their creations; and beseech by obeying the rule of Saint Benedict which states: "Whatever good work you begin to do, beg of God with most earnest prayer to perfect it."

What Stories Are and Why We Read Them

My great-grandfather Frederick Hansen left Denmark with his father, mother, and siblings in 1857. Converts to the Mormon Church, they journeyed by ship and railway until they got to Saint Louis, Missouri, where they loaded their furniture, farm tools, and clothing on handcarts that they intended to haul all the way to the Far West settlement of Zion, which would finally become Salt Lake City, Utah. But Frederick's mother fell ill in Iowa and the wagonmaster suggested she ought to be left there to die. My forebears lost faith in the wagonmaster because of that and, with winter coming on, chose to stay in Iowa, where my great-grandfather farmed until his death in 1932, at the age of eighty-eight, the father of five children. I have seen only one photograph of him: it seems to be a picnic or a family reunion under shade trees and he's a tall, lean, handsome man who's grinning at the camera in a white shirt and suspendered trousers.

I have always imagined we would have gotten along, for earlier, in the late nineteenth century, my great-grandfather had written about the hardships of the handcart trail in The Journal of History, *an article that the family treated like a sacred text, reverently typing and retyping it so each new generation could have a copy. I first became aware of it when I was nine or ten and just discovering the intimate miracle of reading. And now a hunger to write just as he did was fast on its heels. I soon found myself paying greater attention to books, reading them not just for their plots but for hints of who the authors were and why they may have put their words and sentences in an order that only seemed inevitable. If I watched a movie, I would imagine what the scene descriptions and dialogue would have looked like on a page, and if I lamented having, say, a Tarzan episode end, I'd go to the dining room table and write a scene or two of my own sequel, generally concentrating on the prodigy of Johnny Weismuller swinging through the African jungle on strong and convenient vines.*

When I was in the eighth grade at Holy Angels, we were assigned an essay on some element of Christ's Passion, and I raised my hand to ask if I could write it as a short story instead. Sister Pierce, the school principal who taught us, was surprised by the question but could think of no quarrel against it, and so she gave me permission. I have since lost the story, but as I remember it, the point of view was that of a Roman centurion who watched Jesus suffer and die on the cross. It was no better, and possibly no worse, than "Today Is Friday," Ernest Hemingway's story on the same theme. But in choosing to write a fictional version rather than a nonfictional one, I felt I'd made a selection of stunning and eternal importance. I have friends who say a similar thing happened when they crossed an imaginary line and decided they were poets.

Even now, when I'm not writing fiction I miss it. The hankering seems to be analogous to the loss and infertility actors feel when they've been off-stage for a while. Some years ago the Smithsonian Institution asked me to give a talk on a subject of my choosing, and I harkened back to those early experiences as I sought to examine for myself just what it is about stories that makes us need to read or write them.

What Stories Are and Why We Read Them

We fiction readers are questioners. We find ourselves wondering if the facts are right, if a scene truly occurred, what will happen next in the story, and how and where we are being taken. A question we hardly ever ask but perhaps ought to is: "Why are we doing this, anyway?" And to get to that point we'll first have to begin with what stories are.

Story is a hard word to define, especially as I want to use it, that is, in the widest possible way, welcoming whatever kind of prose narrative you can think of, be it the classic short story, or a myth, legend, parable, fairy tale, fable, yarn, novella, novel, or screenplay. A handbook definition of what I'm talking about might go something like this: A story is a fictional narrative about characters in conflict that has meaning for our own lives. Within its confines something happens that effects an important change in the characters, often provoking new insights about themselves or others or the ways of the world. Everything in it is critical to its final unity. Early on in a story we are introduced to a significant problem or tension that only increases with further developments or complications until finally the kettle is filled and it boils over into a crisis. At that point a serious and crucial decision has to be made by the main character or, especially in contemporary stories, the protagonist will arrive at a sudden revelation—what James Joyce identified as an epiphany. Whether given a crisis or an epiphany in the story, we understand that the character has arrived at a turning point in his or her life and, having had that experience, will never be the same, but will think and feel differently in the future. Likewise, we may see the protagonist offered a chance to change but stupidly refuse it. That, too, is crucial. And then there is often a falling off of the action, a resolution where loose ends are tied up, or that relaxation of tensions which is known as the denouement.

A handbook definition, as I said, but it feels too general to be of much help in figuring out what stories are. E. M. Forster isn't far better; he calls a story "a narrative of events arranged in their time sequence—dinner coming after breakfast, Tuesday after Monday, decay after death, and so on. *Qua* story, it can only have one merit: that of making the audience want to know what happens next. And conversely it can only have one fault: that of making the audience *not* want to know what happens next."

The form is so plastic, so endless in its possibilities that it feels foolish to try to describe it. In "Reading," Richard Ford pointed out that the problem with definitions or of looking at stories in terms of their formal features—character, point of view, narrative structure, imagistic pattern, symbol, diction, theme—is that

> Stories and novels . . . are makeshift things. They originate in strong, disorderly impulses; are supplied by random accumulations of life-in-words; and proceed in their creation by mischance, faulty memory, distorted understanding, weariness, deceit of almost every imaginable kind, by luck and by the stresses of increasingly inadequate vocabulary and wandering imagination—with the result often being a straining, barely containable object held in fierce and sometimes inefficient control. . . . And for every writer it's different; different means and expectations, different protocols under which a story accumulates, different temperaments and lingo about how to do it—different work in every way.

In fact, it's far easier to say what a story is not than to say what a story is. True stories are not anecdotes, sketches, character studies, or mood pieces. They are not psychology or sociology or history or biography, though they may adapt elements of all those forms to create their effects. Stories are not about theories or themes, though our high school practice of talking about books in this way often gives people the false impression that serious writers first of all have a point they're trying to prove. What stories try to present is generally sensory, how it feels to fall in love with Romeo or Juliet, to pursue a white whale across the Atlantic, to float in and out of consciousness within view of the snows of Kilimanjaro.

Even if we can't precisely define a story, we know one when we hear one. Take, for example, Isak Dinesen's "The Supper at Elsinore." It begins in this way:

> **Upon the corner of a street of Elsinore, near the harbor, there stands a dignified old gray house, built early in the eighteenth century, and looking down reticently at the new times grown up around it. Through the long years it has been worked into a unity, and when the front door is opened on a day of north-north-west the door of the corridor upstairs will open out of sympathy. Also when you tread upon a certain step of the stair, a board of the floor in the parlor will answer with a faint echo, like a song.**

What may have been a history or a travel article in the first few phrases is abruptly altered when we hear that the house is "looking down reticently at the new times grown up around it," that an upstairs door opens "out of sympathy," that a floorboard answers "like a song." Dinesen frankly tells us in her first paragraph that we are in the land of the tale. She teaches us, as good writers do, how to read her. Even if she were not so fanciful, Dinesen would have had to betray the form fairly soon because the compulsion to create a fictional narrative is at war with the prudence and worries of fact, just as play is at war with duty. Working dogs will herd sheep and fetch mallards and frisbees but only on their terms, without drudgery, with a full measure of fun. And so it is with stories. Otherwise honorable traits like truthfulness and high-mindedness and shock at foul behavior afflict them like food poisoning. T. S. Eliot once said of Henry James that he had a mind so fine that no idea could sully it, a statement often mistakenly thought of as a snide criticism, though in fact Eliot meant that ideology fell to the background when Henry James's fictional characters walked onto the stage.

Early in *The Last Tycoon*, F. Scott Fitzgerald's unfinished novel, a British screenwriter named George Boxley visits the office of the movie tycoon, Monroe Stahr, and sits as if forcibly put there by two invisible attendants.

> Even when he lit a cigarette on Stahr's invitation, one felt that the match was held to it by exterior forces he disdained to control.
>
> Stahr looked at him courteously.
>
> "Something not going well, Mr. Boxley?"
>
> The novelist looked back at him in thunderous silence.
>
> "I read your letter," said Stahr. The tone of the pleasant young headmaster was gone. He spoke as to an equal, but with a faint two-edged deference.
>
> "I can't get what I write on paper," broke out Boxley. "You've all been very decent, but it's a sort of conspiracy. Those two hacks you've teamed me with listen to what I say, but they spoil it—they seem to have a vocabulary of about a hundred words."
>
> "Why don't you write it yourself?" asked Stahr.
>
> "I have. I sent you some."
>
> "But it was just talk, back and forth," said Stahr mildly. "Interesting talk but nothing more."
>
> Now it was all the two ghostly attendants could do to

hold Boxley in the deep chair. He struggled to get up; he uttered a single quiet bark which had some relation to laughter but none to amusement, and said:

"I don't think you people read things. The men are duelling when the conversation takes place. At the end one of them falls into a well and has to be hauled up in a bucket."

He barked again and subsided.

"Would you write that in a book of your own, Mr. Boxley?"

"What? Naturally not."

"You'd consider it too cheap."

"Movie standards are different," said Boxley, hedging.

"Do you ever go to them?"

"No—almost never."

"Isn't it because people are always duelling and falling down wells?"

"Yes—and wearing strained facial expressions and talking incredible and unnatural dialogue."

"Skip the dialogue for a minute," said Stahr. "Granted your dialogue is more graceful than what these hacks can write—that's why we brought you out here. But let's imagine something that isn't either bad dialogue or jumping down a well. Has your office got a stove in it that lights with a match?"

"I think it has," said Boxley stiffly, "—but I never use it."

"Suppose you're in your office. You've been fighting duels or writing all day and you're too tired to fight or write any more. You're sitting there staring—dull, like we all get sometimes. A pretty stenographer that you've seen before comes into the room and you watch her—idly. She doesn't see you, though you're very close to her. She takes off her gloves, opens her purse and dumps it out on a table—"

Stahr stood up, tossing his key-ring on his desk.

"She has two dimes and a nickel—and a cardboard match box. She leaves the nickel on the desk, puts the two dimes back into her purse and takes her black gloves to the stove, opens it and puts them inside. There is one match in the match box and she starts to light it kneeling by the stove. You notice that there's a stiff wind blowing in the window—but just then your telephone rings. The girl picks it up, says hello—listens—and says deliberately into the phone, 'I've never owned a pair of black gloves in my life.' She hangs up, kneels by the stove again, and just as she lights the match, you glance around very suddenly and see that there's another man in the office, watching every move the girl makes—"

Stahr paused. He picked up his keys and put them in his pocket.

"Go on," said Boxley smiling. "What happens?"

"I don't know," said Stahr. "I was just making pictures."

Boxley felt he was being put in the wrong.

"It's just melodrama," he said.

"Not necessarily," said Stahr. "In any case, nobody has moved violently or talked cheap dialogue or had any facial expression at all. There was only one bad line, and a writer like you could improve it. But you were interested."

"What was the nickel for?" asked Boxley evasively.

"I don't know," said Stahr. Suddenly he laughed. "Oh, yes—the nickel was for the movies."

> **The two invisible attendants seemed to release Boxley. He relaxed, leaned back in his chair and laughed.**
>
> **"What in hell do you pay me for?" he demanded. "I don't understand the damn stuff."**
>
> **"You will," said Stahr grinning, "or you wouldn't have asked about the nickel."**

I have often read that passage to my creative writing students on the first day of class because it gets so deftly at the heart of what fiction writers do.

"I was just making pictures," Stahr said. And of course Scott Fitzgerald was making pictures when the screenwriter seemed forced into his chair and his match seemed held to his cigarette by another. But it's Stahr's illustration of sheer storytelling that I particularly want my writing students to pay attention to. We have quite a simple setup: a tired writer in his Hollywood office who is unseen by a pretty stenographer. And we have the fragmentary beginnings of a plot when she furtively pitches her black gloves into a stove and empties her purse on the desktop. We have one plot complication when she lies on the phone, and a further complication when the tired writer notices another man in the room watching every move the stenographer makes. We have a lot of questions, and even some foreboding. When Stahr pauses in his story, we feel the interruption like a tease, and when he confesses he doesn't know where his plot is headed, our disappointment tells us how deeply hooked we were. We may feel duped or toyed with later, but while he held our attention we were elsewhere, and keenly interested, and forgetful of ourselves.

We often have no idea what time it is when we're truly fascinated with our reading. If the fiction writer is particularly good, and his or her world is far different from our own—when we're in the presence, say, of an old-fashioned page-turner—we may be slightly disoriented, even ga-ga, when our non-fictive world makes its sudden and imperious demands. Lostness is, in fact, often what we're after in our reading. Escapist fiction is frequently thought to be the tawdry stuff that our fellow passengers seem to prefer on airplanes, but I have been held as wholly in suspense by Marguerite Duras as by Agatha Christie; I have escaped my life with equal completeness in the fiction of James Lee Burke and P. D. James, or Raymond Carver and Raymond Chandler.

Truth be told, we are not really "escaping," we are "entering into." When he was the fiction editor at *Esquire*, Gordon Lish put together an anthology of stories that he titled *The Secret Life of Our Times*. And that is precisely what stories do: give us access to otherwise hidden, censored, unsayable thoughts and feelings now shiftily disclosed in the guise of plot and character. In the *Star Trek* phrase, it's a mind meld. The hungers of our spirits are fed by sharing in the glimpsed interiority of others.

I have taught screenwriting classes and on the first day asked students to talk about the script they'd like to produce. Usually they have no hard-and-fast ideas about plotting or character yet, but they generally do know how their movie would begin. No one, it seems, is at a loss for a nifty opening: the slow pan along the perfumes and lipsticks on the dressertop, steam rising through a sewer grate as we hear a song by Marilyn Manson, the shot through the chink in a window shade at writhing figures on a four-poster bed. I was surprised that so much attention was paid to what is, after all, just a credit sequence, the last thing shot for many films, until a director explained to me that some people have no firm memories of the movie they've just seen, only of those first few moments when they were, as he put it, "sinking into the dream."

Dreaming does have a lot to do with good storytelling. In fact one thing I've noticed when giving and hearing public readings is that if the fiction's working, if the story's told with authority, there comes a point a few paragraphs in when I find people shifting in their chairs, not from restlessness, I presume, but because they're falling into the dream. We gradually relax in the presence of good prose, we find safety in the proper fictional shape, and we're gently cradled if a plot is familiar enough that we feel slightly ahead of the author—hoping, of course, to be tripped up and surprised. Woefully disappointed when we aren't.

John Gardner taught that great fiction is "a wonderfully simple thing"

> — so simple that most co-called serious writers avoid trying it, feeling they ought to do something more important and ingenious, never guessing how incredibly difficult it is. A true work of fiction does all of the following things, and

> does them elegantly, efficiently: it creates a vivid and continuous dream in the reader's mind; it is implicitly philosophical; it fulfills or at least deals with all of the expectations it sets up; and it strikes us, in the end, not simply as a thing done but as a shining performance.

In his essay "Creative Writers and Day-Dreaming," Sigmund Freud suggested that the pleasure of reading possibly derived from our participation in what is essentially a film from the cinema of another's mind. "But when a creative writer presents his plays to us," he wrote,

> or tells us what we are inclined to take to be his personal day-dreams, we experience a great pleasure, and one which probably arises from the confluence of many sources. The writer softens the character of his egoistic day-dreams by altering and disguising it, and he bribes us by the purely formal—that is, aesthetic—yield of pleasure which he offers us in the presentation of his fantasies . . . Our actual enjoyment of an imaginative work proceeds from a liberation of tensions in our minds. It may even be that not a little of this effect is due to the writer's enabling us thenceforward to enjoy our own day-dreams without self-reproach or shame.

Nightmares and dreams are not meaningless frights and entertainments but unconscious extensions and workings out of our conscious preoccupations. A host of writers have been inspired to produce their creations following especially powerful dreams. Samuel Taylor Coleridge, for example, composed a hundred lines of "Kubla Khan" in his sleep and was dashing them off before he was interrupted by the infamous "person on business from Porlock." John Fowles's vision, or waking dream, of a hooded, melancholy, nineteenth-century woman on the quay at Lyme Regis was, he said, the foremost provocation for *The French Lieutenant's Woman.* Robert Louis Stevenson, whose *Dr. Jekyll and Mr. Hyde* was a product of his feeling that we all have split personalities, confessed it was only "financial fluctuations" that forced him to find a body and vehicle for the subject:

> For two days [Stevenson wrote] I went about racking my brains for a plot of any sort; and on the second night I dreamed the scene at the window, and a scene afterwards split in two, in which Hyde, pursued for some crime, took the powder and underwent the change in the presence of his pursuers.

One contemporary psychologist thinks of our brains as "biological computers with a fabulous bank of software—painfully acquired since birth—and a spectacular degree of flexibility" with programs in them that "must be constantly and regularly revised and updated."

> Sleep is the period when the brain comes off-line, cutting itself off from the sensory input, and restricting psychomotor input. In this off-line period, the great software files of the brain become open and available for revision in the light

of changes that have taken place as the result of the horde of new experiences which occur every day.

With some complex surgery and electrical hookups, Michel Jouvet, a French neurophysiologist, was able to force sleeping cats to perform the stalking, crouching, and pouncing movements the cats would have otherwise *felt* they were doing in those highly active phases of sleep in which dreams are known to occur. Even cats that had never hunted their food went through a full range of predatory exercises as if they were re-running and rechecking their basic programs for survival in order to have them in good working order, just in case.

Nicholas Humphrey of Cambridge University has postulated that in much the same way human beings go through regular tests of their basic programs in social survival. Dreams are, he thinks, "like dress rehearsals for events we can expect, hope for, or fear in everyday life. Situations present themselves in which the dreamer is an actor, playing a part, coping with the often strange twists of the plot, keeping abreast of the unfolding drama."

Which brings us back to story. Aren't they, too, often dress rehearsals for events we can expect, hope for, or fear in everyday life? Aren't they, especially, ways of making chaos orderly and predictable?

In a public television interview with James Dickey and William Price Fox at the University of South Carolina, John

Gardner told his audience, "What happens when you have a really fine character [in fiction] is that you get not only a sense of that kind of person in that kind of town, but yourself and everybody around you. Finally you get a kind of control over the universe, a kind of fearlessness from having understood other people."

In his fine book *The Call of Stories*, Dr. Robert Coles writes of his medical schooling when he often accompanied William Carlos Williams on his rounds. And he marveled at the keen attention Dr. Williams paid to the statements of his patients.

> He could pounce on someone's adjective or verb; he could be delighted in the confounding exception that undoes the seemingly foolproof conclusion. Continuities and discontinuities, themes that appeared and disappeared, references, comparisons, similes and metaphors, intimations and suggestions, moods and mysteries, contours of coherence and spells of impenetrability—he spoke of such matters as he brooded over his life as a doctor, a writer: "We have to pay the closest attention to what we say. What patients say tells us what to think about what hurts them; and what we say tells us what is happening to us—what we are thinking, and what may be wrong with us." A pause, then another jab at my murky mind: "Their story, yours, mine—it's what we all carry with us on this trip we take, and we owe it to each other to respect our stories and learn from them."

We figure out our own lives through fiction. Gail Godwin

once wrote a reminiscence about an unhappy ten-year-old girl whose parents were friends of Gail's. The girl had just been taken out of a fancy private school in Manhattan and was forced to go to a country school where she soon became a pariah. She stayed over at Gail Godwin's house one night, and as Gail was making up the bed in the guestroom she craftily placed a copy of *Jane Eyre* on the bedside table. At breakfast the next morning, the girl asked if she could take the book home and finish it. Even twelve years later that girl, now a mother, was hugely grateful for that story:

> Oh God, [she said,] I loved that book. I LOVED THAT BOOK! You know the part when Jane sneaks up to the room where Helen Burns is dying and gets in bed with her and Helen says, 'Are you warm, darling?' and then they say good night and the next thing that happens is that nice teacher comes in and finds Jane asleep with her arms around the dead girl? I cried and cried. I couldn't stop. I wanted to run to my parents' room and be comforted, but I couldn't, because it was three o'clock in the morning and I had been reading under my covers with a flashlight, which was forbidden. So I just lay there in the dark and sobbed, all by myself.

The tale of Jane Eyre applying for the job of a governess far away from Lowood School became the girl's own story of humiliation and final triumph.

Self-help books provide guidance in the ways that parents

and good advisors do. Stories teach by example, and by permitting us to safely participate in crises we hope to never get near. Quotidian life seldom offers opportunities for glorious heroism or grand agonies of defeat, but fictional entertainments offer those opportunities in abundance. Handbooks on fiction-writing persistently point out that at the climax of the plot the principal characters ought to be confronted with a choice that will be definitive, both in terms of the burgeoning chaos around them and in terms of their own psychologies. Often these are moments of personal reform and redemption, even of metamorphosis, as the hero goes against fate, against his or her upbringing, and becomes wholly different, new. Ethical grayness characterizes much of our human experiences; and we change only incrementally, through a host of seemingly inconsequential decisions. The zest of good storytelling comes from its gross exaggeration of the frightening and mysterious process of change, so that we see heightened in *The English Patient* or *Schindler's List* the horrifying possibilities of wrong choices and the health to ourselves and others in choosing rightly.

Willa Cather once said that first-rate writers cannot be defined, they can only be experienced. She meant that their greatness was not in the formal features of their writing but on the salutary effect their stories have on our hearts and minds. John Gardner wrote that "The great artist, the 'genius,' to use the old-fashioned word, is the [writer] who sees more connections between things than [ordinary people] can see." I finally think our need for stories is our need to find those connections, and to have confirmed for us the theology we hold secret in our heart, that even the least of us are necessary to the great universal plot in ways we hadn't imagined.

A Nineteenth-Century Man

My mother's father divorced his wife before my mother was born. George Sanford Moore, called Sandy. My mother has no memories of him. She stayed with my grandmother, moving from orphanage to farm to wherever there was work until my mother married right after graduation from Sacred Heart High School. With his sons Cleo and Ron—the uncle I was named for—my mother's father shifted around the Midwest, finding whatever jobs he could until he died in Omaha in 1921. When I was a teenager I looked up his obituary in the Omaha World-Herald, *and saw just one line for him: his name and "laborer." I have never even seen his photograph.*

My father's father, Arthur Hansen, lived in Modale, Iowa, in a white one-and-a-half story bungalow that he put together himself from a kit he ordered from the Sears and Roebuck catalog. With his cousin he owned a house-moving company, but his heart wasn't good and he retired before he was sixty in order to concentrate on woodworking. An affable, neat, abstemious man, he never smoked and he would only drink water. My father used to hide his cigarettes and beer from him even after he was married, but my grandfather finally caught on and told his only son that wasn't necessary. I was four when he died and I have few memories of him beyond the fact that he used to delight in hiding from Rob and me when we visited, and we'd run from room to room in his house shouting "Where's Grampa?" until we found him chuckling in a closet or crouched behind a door. We did that a few weeks after his funeral, too, and when I saw the shocked and saddened faces of my family, I finally understood what death was.

The nineteenth century man I write about here was not a blood relative, but the man my mother's mother married late in life. And yet when I hear "grandfather," it is he who comes to mind.

A Nineteenth-Century Man

When I was fourteen and wholly focused on having a career in fine art, I tried my first portrait in oil and turpentine by skidding nails and wrenches away on my dad's basement workbench and setting up next to a screw and bolt drawer a torn, handled, gray-and-white snapshot of my Grandfather Salvador. Grampa had died just a year earlier, in March 1961, at the age of ninety-two, but in honesty I don't remember sorrow and melancholy having much to do with painting him. What I do remember thinking is that here was a face that was easy to do.

He is there now in my widowed mother's apartment, a

handsome and half-bald welterweight staring menacingly from the canvas in his dark galluses and hard-as-porcelain white collar and a purple necktie that looks like the cosmos just after the Big Bang. You do not want to cross that man. My Uncle Dick once said of him, "Dad may have been small but he sure was plainspoken." Short he was, perhaps five-foot-four in his shoes and he shrank with age, but even in his late eighties Frank Salvador was a tough-as-nails, brook-no-guff Colorado rancher with a great gray mustache, high and prominent cheekbones, and an American eagle's frighteningly serious and skeptical eyes. I have seen him in Frederic Remington's paintings of horse soldiers, in Mathew Brady's harrowing pictures of the Civil War, and in the sixteenth-century portraits of Saint Ignatius of Loyola, another hidalgo from the Basque region of Spain.

Was he christened Franco? Francisco? We don't know. We only know that he said he was born April 4, 1869, sailed to America from France, and for a short time settled in Utica, New York, where his mother died in childbirth, and his father, who was deaf, worked the mines until a heavy coal car slammed into him and hacked off both his legs. Knowing there was nothing to do for him, his fellow miners merely took great-grandfather Salvador home to bleed to death hours later in front of his horror-struck son.

My grandfather was seven years old then and suddenly without family. Taken into a Catholic orphanage, he became an altar boy, learned Gregorian chant, and thought about becoming a priest, but then he was sent on an orphan train to Iowa, where foster parents were happy to take on the boys for cheap help around the farm. His foster parents were hateful and poor and his foster mother was insane, though she was not institutionalized for years. Like a waif in a Dickens book, Frank was permitted to go to school only when there were no jobs that needed doing. Which meant rarely. His formal education ended when he turned eleven. And yet he stayed on in their house because he knew how to farm and the Feeleys didn't and his running away would have ruined them. At last, at age twenty-five, he'd had enough and sued them in an Iowa court for his wages. And when he won the judgment, he let them keep their filthy money because he'd "just wanted them to know what was right."

And then he was on his own. When he was in his thirties, he went west with some cattle and tools, and homesteaded a half-section of ranchland near Holyoke, Colorado, and by the 1920s he'd hammered up a fancy two-story house, was threshing his wheat with a Waterloo Boy, taught himself German, arithmetic, and practical science, invented new kinds of cherry trees and tomato plants and a milled and fermented feed for hogs, and hauled his six boys and two girls to town in a glamorous Chandler automobile with jump seats and isinglass windows. Even the names of his children speak of an earlier time: Asa, Dick, Elgin, Cecil, Iona, Harley, Mary Fern, and Percy.

His wife died of pneumonia caused by the great dust bowl of 1935, and for seven years he stayed a widower, until his baby daughter got engaged. And then he went back to Iowa, hunted up my grandmother, his wife's first cousin and the bridesmaid at their wedding, and, in an Old Testament way, married her.

About then he retired from hard farming and whiled away six months of each year in Los Angeles, reading *National Geographic* under the orange and grapefruit trees. And every half year or so the Salvadors would dress up our lives by abruptly driving to our house in Omaha in their deluxe, persimmon-red, Mercury coupe, Grampa's chin raised high from his neck so he could just see over the wheel and hood.

Mrs. Alice Salvador was a beautiful, gracious, tall, *grande dame* with hair as soft and white as a cloud. And Grampa would be there beside her like the queen's shorter pirate, seeming courtly and proud and cantankerous, in highly polished high-button shoes, a gambler's fancy arm garters holding up his shirt-sleeves, and in his hand a red Folger's coffee can that he'd tilt discreetly toward to spit a brown rod of sweetened tobacco juice.

Chewing tobacco was for him the heal-all that aloe and garlic are for others. When I burned my finger, he spit some juice on it, and when I was stung by a bumblebee he took an oozy wad from his mouth and held it on the hot bump on my arm and the sting, indeed, seemed to be sucked away just like he said it would.

Rob and I were twins and Grampa couldn't tell us apart—even my father had trouble back then—so he invented the name Robney for us both, preferring the hint of stutter and second-thought to just plain flat being wrong. We were also the youngest children of a youngest child, so fourscore years separated us from him, and that meant we three were interested in precisely the same things: in getting up at sunrise and talking seriously on the street to astonished strangers and hurrying down to the Kenwood Bakery, our hands in his, to buy white sacks of bear claws and bismarcks for breakfast.

Whenever he strolled with us he told stories: tales about hard-luck ex-soldiers still in their Civil War gray coats, hunting work in the west; about walking twenty miles from town with a fifty-pound sack of flour on his back and the damp green leaf of a paradise tree on his head so he wouldn't faint; about huge pits on his Colorado property where great buffalo herds had instinctively wheeled and churned up dust in order to keep horseflies and pests away; about the James gang genially watering their horses on his foster parents' farm and then, hearing hooves on the road, hurriedly galloping away.

Even when I was nine or ten I thought my grandfather was lying, that his likeliest narratives were no more than yarns; but now, many years later, I know a great deal more about history and the hardships and oddities and the sheer preposterousness of life, and I know how possible it is that whatever he told us was true. And the whole point of his stories was not their truthfulness, after all, but their hidden wisdom about a hazardous world. Like all old men he used the past to defend us from the future.

And how he protected us. He himself couldn't swim and

therefore doubted, truth be told, that anybody could. Hating lakes and hating fishing, but fearing Robney would drown without him, Grampa got into a fat lifejacket and his financier hat and joined us in the motorboat with a bamboo pole that was as tall as he was. When my dad headed toward dark green water, Grampa stopped him with one of his fractious and plainspoken tirades about fish preferring the hotter water you'd find at five feet or less. We trolled, therefore, along the shore, my dad kindly obliging the old guy and nodding hellos to baffled men gassing their engines on the docks as my grandpa halted him now and then to plumb the lake's depth with his bamboo pole and lie about the kinds of fish that liked feeding where children waded.

His sayings were all of the homely sort you'd find in *Poor Richard's Almanac*: "Your word ought to be as good as your signature." "Say what you mean and mean what you say." "Take care of the pennies and the dollars will take care of themselves." And it's for that reason, perhaps, that I have rarely heard him in memory; but I see him all the time: Eating the fat we'd trimmed away from our steaks. Playing Irish jigs on his fiddle with a handkerchief wedged under his chin. Hefting Rob or me up into his lap so we could steer his green Oliver tractor over his cow pasture. Sleeping upright in a dining room chair with his dulled eyes open and slightly rolled back as if he were practicing for death. Kneeling almost reverently to dissect a frail ear of sweetcorn with his knife and see what its problem was.

Wherever he went, he was remembered. Women beamed

when they talked to him. Even powerful men became boys in his company. I have no memories of him ever smiling, but I have keen memories of charmed people blushing and grinning and shaking his hand when Grampa was around. Everything about him was thrilling because he was so thoroughly a nineteenth-century man.

American history is a joy for me whenever the years are his years too. I know things about the Old West simply because I knew him. He is half of Emmett Dalton in *Desperadoes*, there are hints of him in Frank and Jesse in my book about the James gang, and he is as much Atticus Cody as any man I've ever met. I still seem to do portraits of Grampa Salvador from that torn and handled snapshot.

When I write of the past he is present. And so I write of the past.

The Wizard: Remembering John Gardner

In the fall of 1982 I was teaching fiction writing at the University of Michigan and finishing the rough draft of the historical novel that would become The Assassination of Jesse James by the Coward Robert Ford. *A few weeks earlier I'd been a staff member at the Bread Loaf Writer's Conference, where John Gardner heaped such extravagant praise on the manuscript that I wondered if I had* Moby-Dick *on my hands. Artists, like children, Elizabeth Bowen wrote, do their best in an atmosphere of affection and encouragement.*

My habit then, as now, was to write three or four hours in the mornings, run or work out in the gym, then write for two or three hours more, generally quitting around five. My classes were in the evenings. On the afternoon of Tuesday, September 14, I checked the clock just above my desk and considered shutting my sketch book with its many pages of pencilled longhand, for I'd gotten a good four pages done that day, but then I thought, What would John Gardner do? *and I continued on for one more page before I finally got up from the desk after six.*

I went into the living room of my apartment in Ypsilanti, switched on the Sony television, and tuned it to ABC News for some reason. The nightly news was never a habit for me, and ABC would not have been my first choice. And when the screen presented an image it was of the news anchor staring straight at me and announcing—in a weird coincidence that seemed right out of a bad writer's fiction—that novelist John Gardner had been killed that afternoon in a motorcycle accident on a highway in Susquehanna County, Pennsylvania. As gifted a writing teacher as he was a novelist, he'd been riding north from his farm home to meet with a student at the State University of New York at Binghamton, where he founded the creative writing program—and where I would teach six years later.

At first the police said he'd lost control of his black Harley-Davidson after a sharp turn, but that portion of Route 92 was fairly straight, so it seemed more likely he'd swerved to avoid an animal on the roadway and the machine took over, as motorcycles will, veering wildly into a ditch where the handlebar struck him so forcefully in the abdomen that he was rendered unconscious and died of internal bleeding. He was forty-nine years old, the father of two children, and the author of twenty-nine books of fiction, poetry, children's stories, translation, and criticism.

Wednesday morning after his death the sliding glass door to my apartment balcony was open and I smelled John Gardner's Prince Albert pipe tobacco floating in from outdoors. I walked out to the balcony and looked down to the sidewalk, but no one was there.

THE WIZARD: REMEMBERING JOHN GARDNER

When I first arrived at the Iowa Writers Workshop in August 1972, the hot topic was postmodernist fiction and those writers whom Robert Scholes was calling fabulators, such as John Barth, Donald Barthelme, Robert Coover, John Hawkes, and, for many of us, the new kid on the block, John Gardner. *Grendel* was just about a year old then but was still being featured in the Epstein brothers' bookstore in Iowa City, and the novel was in the fast lane of hand-to-hand traffic for those of us who could only afford to share.

A lot of us then were entranced by what Joe David Bellamy called "superfiction": tonic experiments with fable, fairy tale, tall tale, parody, the antimimetic, and the surreal. We felt we were forsaking the tired and pedestrian ways of thinking and writing that seemed to have gotten Americans mired in Vietnam and shifted American fiction into a pallid and hopelessly weak position below journalism. We'd tried realism and found television could do it better. We favored, therefore, hallucination and incantation, fun and games with form and genre, frustrations of chronology and logic that were possibly born of the late sixties' fascination with mind-altering drugs.

Grendel was a fresh, funny, and fashionably metafictional reworking of the Old English epic *Beowulf* from the perspective of a hideous monster that Gardner hoped our psyches would recognize as a familiar, and whose seething rage was, for Gardner, only the natural outgrowth of taking seriously the futility and nihilism of Jean-Paul Sartre's philosophy. Still his most popular book among writers, *Grendel* affected us then with its allusiveness and finesse, its intricate architecture and style, its shrewd unifying of *Frankenstein* and Aristotle, Franz Kafka and J. R. R. Tolkien, William Blake and Walt Disney. We missed on first reading, I think, his fierce commentary on the twentieth century's spiritual and psychological decay, and because we missed it Gardner would have to write the jeremiad *On Moral Fiction*.

John Gardner was just thirty-eight then but he was already famous in a town fascinated by gossip, legends, and writerly news, whether informed or not. We knew he'd gotten his Ph.D. in Medieval Literature at Iowa, but few knew that he'd satisfied his dissertation requirements with a still-unpublished novel called *The Old Men*; and there was talk that he'd formerly been a visiting student in the Writers Workshop, but had turned in fiction that was so offputting to his dreary peers that he fell into despair and absented himself from further classes, and now felt such loathing for the place that he wouldn't even offer a reading there. Wouldn't even return telephone calls, some people said. That, of course, inflated his reputation among the workshop's graduate students, who regularly appealed to get John Gardner there and just as regularly forgave him for his rejections.

A thirty-year-old John Irving was teaching both *The Wreckage of Agathon* and *Grendel* in his "Forms of Fiction" classes at Iowa. Stanley Elkin, who was a visiting professor, told a story about running into the Gardners in New York City where Gardner had reportedly signed a three-book contract with Alfred A. Knopf for two hundred thousand dollars. Equivalent to one million now. Elkin told us the Gardners were trying to rent a car in Manhattan and having no luck so they'd simply asked where the nearest Mercedes-Benz dealership was, walked to it, and purchased a sedan on the spot.

We were thrilled by such stories. Even then penniless writers kept themselves at the hard and sometimes dispiriting work of fiction writing by obsessing on the great publishing score. And that Gardner accomplished it while producing fabulous, witty, scholarly, sly postmodernist fictions made him a hero and exemplar for us.

I took my own first trip to the East with a girlfriend and fellow graduate student just after *The Sunlight Dialogues* was published. I still couldn't afford a hardback, but I'd house-sat Colin and Brendan Irving while their father and mother went to New York, and John Irving repaid me with a hot-off-the-presses edition of Gardner's book. My Volkswagen had no radio so my girlfriend and I took turns reading *The Sunlight Dialogues* to each other, and as it was a 673-page book, it lasted all the way to New York and halfway back.

If *Grendel* was new fabulism, *The Sunlight Dialogues* was Chaucerian realism, an ingenious homage to the strategies of the great nineteenth-century novels written by Herman Melville, Leo Tolstoy, and Henry James, with just a hint of the magical realism of Gabriel Garciá Márquez's *One Hundred Years of Solitude.* In it an old police chief in Batavia, New York, a good man of feeling and firm ideals who seems an affable oaf from a Walt Disney cartoon, has conversations and magical encounters in jail with a wild-eyed Cain whose fall from grace has turned him into an anarchist. It is a zestful but sometimes difficult book, full of philosophy and omens, one that its flapjacket called "a world-size novel in which the complex life of an American small town is perceived as an all-encompassing medieval romance in modern dress, a pathless forest for twentieth-century knights, ladies, and wizards." Gardner's first bestseller, it was also the foremost expression of his governing metaphysical system, one that Professor Greg Morris used to title his critical study of Gardner's fiction: *A World of Order and Light.* Capacious and cautiously optimistic, it was a surprising book for some of those who liked *Grendel* for the wrong reasons—Who *is* this guy? they may have thought—but following that first hit with one that was both popular and affirmative and formidably ambitious made Gardner a major contemporary author.

We finished *The Sunlight Dialogues* just outside Carbondale, where Gardner was then teaching at Southern Illinois University, and as we passed first one Carbondale exit and another and another we entertained notions of looking him up at his farm on Boskydell Road. I was finally too shy. I held his work in such awe that I was intimidated, I feared looking like a fool as I gushed about his originality and blushingly thanked him for his fiction. I had little idea then of how forgiving novelists are of flattery or how willing they are to befriend those who idolize them.

My picture of John Gardner then was that of Jill Krementz's flapjacket photograph: a handsome man with fashionably long white hair, holding a pipe to his mouth as he solemnly stared off in the distance. He seemed aloof and stern, even tortured, a fine-tuned intellectual who would not suffer fools gladly, whose household possibly buffered him from the world as he furiously filled reams of paper with his prose.

That picture held force for me until 1979 when I first attended the Bread Loaf Writers' Conference in Vermont. My first novel, *Desperadoes*, had just been published that April and my old friend John Irving—now suddenly rich and famous following the publication of *The World According to Garp*—nominated me to be invited up to the conference as a fellow and to work with him in his classroom sections. Teaching there, too, was John Gardner.

William Kennedy had fittingly called him "the Lon Chaney of contemporary fiction," and he was that in spades, a charming shape-shifter, unpredictable, even perverse in his choices, as capable of a pastoral as he was an epic romp. *Jason and Medeia* and *Nickel Mountain* and *The King's Indian* and *October Light* and who-knew-what-else? were in print by then and he was tirelessly producing other books—fifteen volumes of poetry and prose appeared between 1974 and 1980—as if it were no harder to write them than read them. My first night in Treman, a kind of summer cottage saloon where the faculty hung out following the nightly public readings, I watched Gardner from a distance, intimidated and menaced by his talent and output, and content to wing talk about film options, foreign rights, and the flotsam of book publishing with the other hustling upstarts there, a kind of greeting ritual like that practiced in harp seal herds. (Stanley Elkin, upon overhearing us, whined, "Oh! My ca-reer! My ca-reer!") But when I spied Gardner chatting with Shyla Irving by the kitchen refrigerator, I finally got up the courage to oh so casually stroll over.

Shyla introduced me to Gardner first as their *au pair* in Iowa and then as the author of *Desperadoes*. And to my astonishment and thrilled affection, Gardner smiled hugely and said he'd read the novel and liked it. "I kept turning the pages, thinking *He's going to make a mistake*. But you *didn't*."

I have no memory of our first conversation beyond his mention of my novel—I'd gotten what I wanted, I could go home now. Wonderfully generous to younger writers, Gardner generally tried to read as many first novels as he could, and generally found reason to praise them. Earnestness was important to Gardner—it was the foundation for his famous dictum that fine literature offered "a vivid and continuous dream" as well as "a stirring performance"—and earnestness is typically not in short supply among first novelists. We all struck him as promising, but he found genius in only a hundred or so. "You're the best writer up here," he once told me at Bread Loaf, and I haven't had the heart to find out whom else he'd tried to inspire that way.

Ebullient, hearty, full of energy and zest, he teased, he yarned, he winked without winking; he was like the characters of fun and mischief in his own children's books, or a facetious Merlin, a Chaucerian rascal, a Welsh serf pleasantly stunned to be serving at the king's pleasure. Wearing heavy biker boots, a wrinkled blue chambray shirt, the kind of navy blue khakis that are commonly issued to janitors, and the kind of goldish brown corduroy jacket that seems sold only to those in English departments, he was the unkempt contradiction of styles that we expect our novelists to be. He was wide as a farmer just off a tractor, hale as a regular at the truckstop cafe. He seemed to perpetually hold a fireless pipe in his hand, and tamping the pipe's ashes with his first finger had made the nail black with soot. His hair was shockingly white and hung as sleek and long as a forties vamp's, and there were tales that he was one of those whose hair had gone gray overnight, or seemed to, a flag of the guilt he felt for killing his brother Gilbert—the horrible tractor accident and its aftermath that was brilliantly detailed, if altered, in his short story "Redemption." I have also heard people say that he never slept, meaning *never.* And that he read three books a day. And drank straight gin in a waterglass while writing. Exactly the sort of gossip that he may have fostered himself. (Gardner once told me he figured out that it was easiest to write and teach if he taught Old English, and that he'd gone on to learn twenty-seven languages. When I asked him about that a night later—

"Twenty-*seven*, John?"—he grinned and said, "Did I tell you that? Don't believe half of what I say.") Gardner forgot nothing of what he read and seemed to get the sense of a page in an instant. He was a fast talker, fond of slang, a hint of Manhattan in his voice though he'd grown up in Batavia; and his mind seemed even faster, as if we all were at half-speed and his hardest discipline was patience—*heard it, seen it, read it, done it* hardly hidden behind his smile. His soft blue eyes seemed friendly and amused, fatherly in their sympathy, so it was often a surprise to a few that he could be as blunt and damning as a hammer.

Gardner was overly fond of grandiose statements that intentionally got the hackles up. At one conference he mentioned that there were only three plots: boy meets girl, a stranger rides into town, a hero goes off in pursuit of adventure. When someone objected that Virginia Woolf's *Mrs. Dalloway* hardly fit that scheme, he said, "Well, that's why she's boring." Good-natured arguments were his favorite party game—he was lawyerly in his facility at changing sides—and he was aghast when people harbored grudges over stances he'd taken up just for the fun of it.

Alfred Kazin once referred to him as a "beautifully educated" man, and that odd adverb may have had its basis in Gardner's familiarity with classical and medieval literature and philosophy, with all those books we wish we could say we've read but don't truly want to open. To hear him talk at parties was often dizzying; look into his many one-on-one interviews and you have a sense of the high intellectual acumen and sheer wealth of learning that Gardner brought to his most genial conversations.

We were all cowed by it. My favorite story about him took place at an academic dinner party with a physicist, a poet, and an expert on opera. Each held forth on his or her specialty and Gardner responded so knowledgeably it seemed he'd majored in the subject; and then he headed into frontiers where he seemed better informed than the professionals were, naming fascinating new theories and compositions that, he politely implied, they really *ought* to have been acquainted with. Embarrassed by the amateur, the experts humbled themselves home and only after prolonged investigations found out that Gardner had been making everything up, he'd simply been practicing some academic vaudeville to keep himself interested.

My first summer in Vermont was followed by others on the conference staff, assisting Gardner in his seminars. His popularity as a teacher meant that he filled the Little Theater at Bread Loaf and that the free-ranging discussions of form and technique that were typical of other fiction-writing groups of twenty or thirty members were often impossible for his own crowds. He opted instead for sessions in which the participants were instructed to imitate the famous styles of writers like William H. Gass or Erica Jong in retelling the tale of the three little pigs; or he'd simply have them construct a plot and tell it. Gardner would hear it out and render a quick judgment of its probabilities for success. Most of the plots were hackneyed or based too strictly on firsthand experience—nurse stories, separation stories, stories of persecution, stories of being misunderstood—and Gardner was merciless at exposing those faults and the bathos they would produce. Yet he was good, too, at finding the authenticity in a piece, at fitting it into a genre where it rightly belonged, at congratulating stories that were well begun. Crushed, some people were, but a great many more were honestly corrected and encouraged.

And that was particularly true of his one-on-one manuscript conferences. Was anyone not hailed and lauded in those sessions? I looked at one participant's story and found overfamiliar phrasing, a tawdry plot, and howlers in the imagery; I had a hard time even flattering the author for her typing. Gardner looked at that story and found a twangy prose equivalent of honky-tonk country music that no writer had ever tried before. "You're doing something brand *new* here," he told the rather talentless woman. She floated from her talk with him.

Gardner regularly handled a huge load of student manuscripts in the twelve filled days of Bread Loaf, and not just the fifty pages allotted from each participant but the whole book. I'd see him happily teeter up to his room with a heavy stump of prose and then later hunch over the books with the writers and treat them to the serious attention they'd probably never have again. Even though he wasn't required to tutor me, he asked to read 480 pages of my work-in-progress on *The Assassination of Jesse James by the Coward Robert Ford* and just a half day later offered wonderfully cogent and thorough suggestions on how the book could be improved—even while he proclaimed it "brilliant." I hoped God would see me as Gardner did. If Gardner spent compliments like pennies, there was no tarnish on them; if I felt intoxicated by his flattery, there was no hangover in which his praise seemed magnified, false, or condescending; he seemed honestly amazed by the strangeness and multifariousness in the stories of others, possibly because his own fantastic imagination helped him to fully immerse himself in their quite different worlds.

Gardner was just finishing *Mickelsson's Ghosts* at the time; it was a huge block of white paper in his room and his hope of finally getting out of the financial chaos his life had become. A bleak despondency had so invaded him periodically that he wrote *In the Suicide Mountains* in 1974 to kill off the notion of killing himself. And now he said the Internal Revenue Service was hounding him for three hundred thousand dollars in back taxes; he was frankly losing interest in teaching; he'd nearly died of a cancer; his first marriage had failed, and his second.

Mickelsson's Ghosts was a great but much-maligned novel. Gardner had written too much too fast too carelessly for him not to have garnered some hostility from reviewers, and *Mickelsson's Ghosts* was just the handiest target for the antagonisms that *On Moral Fiction* engendered and the offenses inflicted by such strangely ill-considered products as *The Life and Times of Chaucer*, for which he was accused of plagiarism, and *Freddy's Book*, a minor novel that seemed just a busy writer's make-work.

Mickelsson was, at that time, a perfect exemplar of himself: a Christian humanist philosopher of ethics in flight from the university and in pursuit of Eden and a fresh start in life in a Pennsylvania farmhouse that turns out to be haunted by the past. It's a grand kitchen sink of a book, a ghost story, a psychological thriller, a sentimental pastoral, full of ideas and subjects and wild ambition, but it's about love as few other books truly are, and the generosity of feeling in it, its *caritas* and affirmation of life in all its happiness and horror make it, with *Grendel* and *The Sunlight Dialogues*, one of Gardner's most serious and important novels.

Whether he had a sense of that wasn't clear to me in August 1982. We were again at Bread Loaf and rooming on the same floor in a three-story house called Maple. Gardner was getting married to Susan Thornton in September and was pleased that I would be attending the Rochester, New York, wedding that tragically became his funeral in Batavia. We talked of death a good deal that summer, but that only loomed in importance *ex post facto*. We talked about politics, too—he was a Republican—and his hopes for his still-unfinished novel, *Shadows*. (The children's book I'd just finished was called, quite unconsciously, *The Shadowmaker*, and the character of the wizard in it was in some ways a sketch of John.)

And one evening I heard the screen door bang shut on the second-floor porch and looked up to see Gardner outside with his pipe, watching people stroll the green hayfields in the soft golden twilight of Vermont. I went out to chat with him and he turned, and I saw that his trousers were darkly stained with a wide spill of some kind and he was airing them out. Chagrin might have changed other men's faces in that circumstance, but Gardner's features were filled with a kind of forbearance of all ills and distress. His wonderful smile held a trace of irony, but mostly there was humor and radiance in it, as if this too was life on earth and he would be more than tolerant of it—he would heed it, own it, seek it, and finally celebrate it, just as he had in his fiction.

The Pilgrim:
Saint Ignatius of Loyola

I have spent more than a third of my life in Jesuit schools as either a student or teacher, and my brother was a member of the Wisconsin Province of the Society of Jesus for nine years, so when I visited Rome in 1989 and found myself in Saint Peter's Square, I got directions to the religious order's international headquarters on Borgo Sancto Spiritu.

I thought at first I'd just look up some of the handwritten documents of Ignatius of Loyola in the library, but when there I found out the head librarian was my former Latin teacher at Creighton University, Fr. Joseph Costello. We were chatting about old times and my writing projects when he informed me that Saint Ignatius's fourth-floor rooms in the house next to the Church of the Gesù were being restored by a California Jesuit named Tom Lucas. Not being shy about such things, I got Fr. Lucas's phone number and called him, and he graciously took me on a private tour.

Workers were tearing out two ornate altars, each seeming as big as a

Buick, that had been installed in Ignatius's bedroom and office and guest parlor over the centuries, and the other accretions of reverence that would not have been there when that was his home were being stripped away. The floor was being covered with sixteenth-century tiles that Tom had found above the ceiling, and the plain, wooden furniture that Ignatius used was finding its place again. Although not yet finished when I was there, the final look, it was clear, would be Spartan. But it was the saint's clothing that gave me the greatest sense of who Ignatius was: Like my grandfather, a fellow Basque, he was a wiry little man whose clean but much worn black cassock was repaired many times with stitching, and whose shined but unadorned black house shoes seemed those of a boy and were no larger than my hand. Holding them was a lesson in his humility and holiness, his intensity and toughness. At once I felt the tenderness one feels for a friend who's died. And when, a few years later, Paul Elie contacted me to write about a favorite saint for his anthology A Tremor of Bliss: Contemporary Writers on the Saints, *I had no hesitation about whom I would choose.*

THE PILGRIM: SAINT IGNATIUS OF LOYOLA

More than two hundred miracles were attributed to Ignatius of Loyola when the judges for the cause of his canonization, the Rota, assembled their sixteen hundred witness statements in 1622. A surgeon held a signature of Ignatius to his head and his headaches and sight problems ended. A Franciscan nun's broken femur was healed when a Spanish priest applied a patch of Ignatius's clothing to her thigh. A Spanish woman held a picture of Ignatius to her hugely swollen stomach and was soon cured of dropsy. Juana Clar, of Manresa, was gradually losing her sight until she got down on her knees and permitted a fragment of Ignatius's bones to be touched to her eyelids. She felt at once such pleasure that it was as if, she said, she'd seen fresh roses. Within a day her pain went away and her vision was perfectly restored. And so on.

Even though I presume those stories are true, I find myself oddly unaffected by them; it's as if I heard that Saint Ignatius, like Cool Hand Luke, could eat fifty eggs. I have read every major biography and book about Ignatius, I have held his shoes in my hands, I have walked through his freshly restored rooms in the house next to what is now the Church of the Gesù, and I have next to me as I write this a nail that was in one of the walls. Supernatural prodigies have nothing to do with my rapt and consuming interest in him. I have simply been trying to figure out how to live my life magnificently, as Ignatius did, who sought in all his works and activities the greater glory of God.

Iñigo López de Loyola was born in the Loyola castle in 1491, the last son of thirteen children born of a wealthy and highly esteemed family in Azpeitia in the Basque province of Guipúzcoa. His father, Beltrán de Loyola, died in 1507, but we do not know when his mother, Marina Sánchez de Licona, died, only that she predeceased her husband; it's highly probable she died in the child's infancy, for Iñigo was nursed by María de Garín, a neighboring blacksmith's wife, who later taught him his prayers and with whose children he played.

Guipúzcoa means "to terrify the enemy" and there was a huge, legendary emphasis on fearlessness and aggressiveness among the region's men. Juan Pérez, the oldest of Iñigo's brothers, joined a ship's escort for Christopher Columbus and finally died heroically in the Spanish conquest of Naples, and another brother, Hernando, gave up his inheritance in order to go to the Americas, where he disappeared in 1510. In fact, of Iñigo's seven older brothers, only one was not a conquistador or fighting man. That brother, Pero López, took holy orders and became rector of the Church of San Sebastián at Azpeitia; and his father may have sought holy orders for Iñigo as well, for he was enrolled in preseminary studies in the arts of reading and writing before he was sent, at the age of thirteen and probably at his own behest, to acquire the skills and manners of a courtier in the household of his father's friend, the chief treasurer of King Ferdinand of Castile.

His fantasies became those of intrigue and gallantry and knightly romance. Of him in his twenties it was written: "He is in the habit of going round in cuirass and coat of mail, wears his hair long to the shoulder, and walks about in a two-colored, slashed doublet with a bright cap." We have evidence that he was cited in court for brawling, and he himself confessed that "he was a man given over to the vanities of the world; with a great and vain desire to win fame he delighted especially in the exercise of arms." We have no evidence from him of his affairs of the heart beyond his furtive confession that he was "fairly free in the love of women" and, later, that he often spent hours "fancying what he would have to do in the service of a certain lady, of the means he would take to reach the country where she was living, of the verses, the promises he would make to her, the deeds of gallantry he would do in her service. He was so enamored with all this that he did not see how impossible it would all be, because the lady was of no ordinary rank"; indeed, she seems to have been Doña Catalina, the glamorous sister of Emperor Charles V and future queen of John III of Portugal.

When his employer, the king's treasurer-general, died in 1517, the twenty-six-year old Iñigo found another friend and benefactor in the viceroy of Navarre, who hired him as his "gentleman," a kind of factotum or righthand man. Iñigo de Loyola was a finished hidalgo by then, a haughty Lothario and swashbuckler, famous for his flair and charm and machismo, his fastidiousness and fondness for clothes, his highly educated politeness and chivalry and hot temper, his ferocity of will, his fortitude and loyalty—his Basqueness, as the Spanish would say—and also his acuity and craft in negotiations, his penetrating stare, his photographic memory, his fine penmanship, his reticence and precaution in speech, his love of singing and dancing. Like his Spanish friends, he was religiously naive, and Catholicism seems to have been rather perfunctory for him—high-table rituals without flourish or kisses. "Although very much attached to the faith," a friend and biographer wrote, "he did not live in keeping with his belief, or guard himself from sin: he was particularly careless about gambling, affairs with women, and duelling."

Iñigo was not a professional soldier then, as he'd fancied he'd be, but a public administrator, "a man of great ingenuity and prudence in worldly affairs and very skillful in the handling of men, especially in composing difficulties and discord." But in May 1521, his skillfulness in the handling of men put Iñigo alongside the magistrate of Pamplona in Navarre, defending its fortress in the midst of a huge French offensive on the region along the Pyrenees that the Spanish king had annexed five years earlier. We have no idea how many citizens were with Iñigo, but there could not have been more than a handful holding out against a highly trained French force of three hundred. Late in the nine-hour siege of the fortress, an artillery shot crashed between Iñigo's legs, shattering the right and harming the other. After he fell, the fortress surrendered, and the French made it a point of chivalry to treat Iñigo with such exemplary kindness it may have seemed a form of sarcasm. Their finest physicians operated on him and graciously hospitalized him for a fortnight in his own Pamplona residence before hauling him forty miles northwest to Azpeitia on a litter.

In his family's castle Iñigo's fever and illness grew worse, and village surgeons decided the skewed bones of his leg would have to be broken again and reset—without anesthetic. Even thirty years later he would describe that agony as "butchery," but he was fiercely determined to give no "sign of pain other than to clench his fists." When finally his right leg healed, Iñigo realized that it was foreshortened and that the fibula had knitted jaggedly so that an ugly jutting was just under his knee. Still thinking of finding fame in royal courts and of striding forth in fashionably tight leggings and knee-high boots, he made himself "a martyr to his own pleasure" and underwent the horrific ordeal of having the offending bone chiseled and shaved away.

And then a change began to occur in him. While lying about and suffering further treatments that failed to lengthen his brutalized leg, he sought books of medieval chivalry to read. Surprisingly, the only books available in the Loyola mansion were a four-volume *Vita Jesu Christi* by Ludolph of Saxony and a kind of dictionary of saints called *Flos Sanctorum* by Jacopo da Varazze. With a sigh he read even those. A confidant later overstated the situation by writing of Iñigo that "he had no thought then either of religion or of piety," but it can be fairly said that his simple, unreflective, folk Christianity had not forced him to take his life here seriously nor to compare himself to the holy men of the past, whom Ludolph of Saxony called knightly followers of Christ—*caballeros imitadores*. Speaking of himself in the third person in his autobiography, Ignatius put it this way:

> As he read [the books] over many times, he became rather fond of what he found written there. Putting his reading aside,

> **he sometimes stopped to think about the things he had read and at other times about the things of the world that he used to think about before. . . . Our Lord assisted him, causing other thoughts that arose from the things he read to follow these. While reading the life of Our Lord and of the saints, he stopped to think, reasoning within himself, "What if I should do what St. Francis did, what St. Dominic did?" So he pondered over many things that he found to be good, always proposing to himself what was difficult and serious, and as he proposed them, they seemed to him easy to accomplish.**

We are challenged by Ignatius in much the same way that he was challenged by Francis and Dominic. And that may be the best purpose for books of saints: to have our complacency and mediocrity goaded, and to highlight our lame urge to go forward with the familiar rather than the difficult and serious. We often find tension and unease with the holy lives we read about because there is always an implicit criticism of our habits and weaknesses in greatness and achievement. We know God wants us to be happy, but what is happiness? What is enough? What is the difference between that which is hard to do and that which ought not be done by me? Women are often put off or mystified by this highly masculine saint, but I find so many points of intersection with Iñigo's life that I feel compelled to ask, What if I should do what Ignatius did? And it does not seem to me easy to accomplish.

Iñigo was thirty years old, which was far older then than

now, and yet he found himself wrought up by questions about his purpose on earth that his friends had put a halt to as teenagers. But he was helped in his religious crisis by his discovery of affective patterns to his inner experience, a discovery that would later form the basis for the "Rules for Discernment of Spirits" in his *Spiritual Exercises*.

> When he was thinking about the things of the world, he took much delight in them, but afterwards, when he was tired and put them aside, he found that he was dry and discontented. But when he thought of going to Jerusalem, barefoot and eating nothing but herbs and undergoing all the other rigors that he saw the saints had endured, not only was he consoled when he had these thoughts, but even after putting them aside, he remained content and happy. . . . Little by little he came to recognize the difference between the spirits that agitated him, one from the demon, the other from God.

Concluding that he ought to change radically, Iñigo chose to give up his former interests and pursuits, and, on a pilgrimage to Jerusalem, undergo the hard penances for his sins that "a generous soul, inflamed by God, usually wants to do." Confirmation of that choice came one August night in his sickroom when he was graced with a clear and tremendously consoling image of Our Lady with the Infant Jesus, "and he was left with such loathing for his whole past life and especially for the things of the flesh, that it seemed that all the fantasies he had previously pictured in his mind were driven from it." Even his family noted the difference in him and, far from thinking him crazy, seemed inspired by his faith and good example. Seeing that Iñigo wanted to go even farther in his religious life, however, Martín García de Loyola took his limping brother from room to room in the grand old house, pointing out the jasper and furnishings and fine tapestries, and appealing to him to "consider what hopes had been placed in him and what he should become . . . all with the purpose of dissuading him from his good intention."

But Iñigo was not budged. He filled three hundred pages of a blank account book with extracts from the Gospels and his readings, found a picture of Our Lady of Sorrows and a book of hours of Our Lady, fitted himself out like a knight-errant, and finally left the Loyola house in late February 1522. Offering farewells to his sister Magdalena at Anzuola and to his former employer, the viceroy of Navarre, in Navarrete, he went eastward on his mule another two hundred miles to the Benedictine monastery of Montserrat in Catalonia. After a full, general confession of his past life in writing, which took three days, Iñigo gave up his fine clothes to a tramp, put on a penitential sackcloth tunic and rope-soled sandals, and on the eve of the Annunciation of Our Lady observed a knightly vigil-at-arms at the feet of the Black Madonna, where he vowed perpetual chastity and left his flashing sword and dagger in the shrine. Effectively, his former life was over.

Barcelona was the port of embarkation for Rome where,

through agreement with the Turks, pilgrims were given permission to go to the Holy Land by the pope himself at Easter. But Adrian of Utrecht, the new pope-elect, was himself in Spain and on his slow way to the port, and Iñigo was at pains to avoid his old friends in the Navarrese nobility, whom he rightly presumed would be part of Adrian's retinue. So he went from Montserrat to Manresa, a few miles north, with the intention of staying perhaps three days, but the affective experience of God he felt there was so powerful that Iñigo stayed in Manresa almost a year, a period he later thought of as "my primitive Church."

To vanquish his vanity there, Iñigo let his nails go untrimmed and his hair and beard grow full and wild as nests, and as he tilted from door to door for food and alms in his prickly tunic, he found joy and sweetness in the jeering of children who called him "*El hombre saco*"—Old Man Sack. He helped with the poor and sick in the hospital of Santa Lucia, finding no task offensive, and primarily resided in a Dominican friary, though he often withdrew to a hermit's cave in the hillsides above the river Cardoner. Eating no meat and drinking no wine, fasting until he was little more than skin and skeleton, ill and sleepless much of the time, flagellating himself for his sins, Iñigo was nevertheless an Olympian at prayer, attending Matins with the Dominicans, and Mass, Vespers, and Compline in the cathedral where the canons regular chanted the office in Latin, of which he knew not a word. Exhausting as that regimen might have been, he gave a full seven hours more to kneeling at prayer and, if he found a peseta of free time, read to the point of memorization *The Imitation of Christ* by Thomas à Kempis, a book he would later call "the partridge among spiritual books." And yet, as he says in his autobiography,

> Sometimes he found himself so disagreeable that he took no joy in prayer or in hearing mass or in any other prayer he said. At other times exactly the opposite of this came over him so suddenly that he seemed to have thrown off sadness and desolation just as one snatches a cape from another's shoulders. Here he began to be astounded by these changes that he had never experienced before, and he said to himself, "What new life is this that we are now beginning?"

Compared to his former life as a grand hidalgo, it seemed to have no purpose, and he was so further anguished by his infirmities, fasts, mortifications, and scruples that he found it hard to imagine going on as he had and was assailed with the urge to kill himself, fear of offending God being the one thing that held him back. But gradually Iñigo figured out—possibly with the help of his Benedictine confessor—that he'd simply gone too far, and he gently tempered his penances in obedience, he thought, to the promptings of a Holy Being who was treating him, as he said, "just as a schoolmaster treats a child whom he is teaching."

Enlightenment came to him on the foremost aspects of Catholic orthodoxy, of the Holy Trinity functioning like three harmonious keys in a musical chord, of how God created the world from white-hot nothing, of how Christ was really present in the Eucharist; and frequently over the next few years he saw the humanity of Christ and Our Lady, giving him "such strength in his faith that he often thought to himself: if there were no Scriptures to teach us these matters of the faith, he would be resolved to die for them, only because of what he had seen." And one famous day on the banks of the Cardoner, the pilgrim, as he habitually called himself, was graced with an illumination of such great clarity and insight about "spiritual things and matters of faith and of learning" that "he seemed to himself to be another person and had an intellect other than he had before." Testimony to the great learning Iñigo seemed to have acquired, as he said, *de arriba*, from above, was provided later by Martial Mazurier, a professor of theology at the Sorbonne, who asserted "that never had he heard any man speak of theological matters with such mastery and power."

Because he often referred to his Cardoner illumination as the foundation of all that he would later do, it has been argued that Iñigo was given foreknowledge then and there of the Society of Jesus that would be formally instituted in 1540, but far more likely was it the origin of Iñigo's shift from a worried, isolated, flesh-despising penitent to a far more tranquil and outgoing man who was less concerned with harsh penances than he was with Christ-like service to others.

Essential elements of his *Spiritual Exercises*—finally published in 1548—were probably composed in Manresa about this time.

Influenced in part by Ludolph of Saxony's *Vita Jesu Christi*, the Abbot of Montserrat's *Ejercitatorio de la vida espiritual*, and *Meditationes vitae Christi* by a fourteenth-century Franciscan, the *Spiritual Exercises* fashioned for the first time what is now popularly known as a retreat. The handbook offered spiritual directors a practical and systematic method of having retreatants meditate, in silence and solitude over an intensive four-week span, on God's plan in the creation of human beings, humanity's fall from grace through sin, the gifts of humility and poverty, and the glory of the life, passion, and resurrection of Jesus. Each psychologically astute meditation gently guided a retreatant to choose a fuller Christian life and, as the author himself had done, "to overcome oneself, and to order one's life, without reaching a decision through some disordered affection."

Early in the *Spiritual Exercises* practitioners are told to reflect on themselves and ask: "What have I done for Christ? What am I doing for Christ? What ought I to do for Christ?" Iñigo's own reply to that final question was to complete his long-delayed pilgrimage to Jerusalem. *El hombre saco* was by then affectionately being called *El hombre sancto*, the Holy Man, and when in the hard winter he forsook his tunic and sandals for a family's gift of shoes and beret and two brown doublets, the family preserved his sackcloth as a holy relic. Refusing alms that were offered from friends—possibly because they themselves were in such great want—Iñigo left Manresa on foot in late February 1523, and stayed in Barcelona twenty days, going from door to door to beg for food and provisions for his journey and so impressing Isabel Roser with his talk of God and religion that she paid for his sea passage to Rome and remained his principal benefactor throughout his life.

Whoever met him seems to have liked him; he found no trouble getting an apostolic blessing for his pilgrimage in Rome from Adrian VI, the former Spanish prime minister, nor finding free passage on ships in Venice and Cyprus, and on September 4, Iñigo walked into the Holy City in the midst of a huge procession of Christians and Egyptian Jews. He hoped to never leave.

Palestine was then fiercely held by Turkish Muslims, whose Christian go-betweens were Franciscan friars. After following a highly regulated program of pilgrimages to the Holy Sepulcher, Bethany, Bethlehem, and the Jordan, Iñigo's fervor was such that he approached a friar and told him of his plan to stay on in the city where Jesus had walked, continually venerating the holy sites and helping souls. But he was forbidden that option by the friar's superior, who feared the Spanish crusader would be killed by the Turks. In fact, five hundred Turkish cavalrymen freshly arrived from Damascus were truculently prowling the city and the panicked governor of Jerusalem was urging the pilgrims to leave. After hurried last looks at Christ's footprints on the Mount of Olives, for which he paid the Turkish guards a pen-knife and scissors, Iñigo obediently left with the other pilgrims for Europe, hoping to find his way to Jerusalem again, but preferring, for the time being, to immerse himself in philosophical and theological studies.

To do that he would need Latin. Hence he withstood the hazards of four months of shipboard travel to go back to Spain, where Isabel Roser furnished the little that Iñigo needed while he was taught, gratis, by a professor of Latin grammar at the University of Barcelona. His life there was full of self-imposed hardships: he slept on the plank floor of a friend's garret room, walked about in shoes that had no soles, and begged food for the poor while subsisting himself on plain bread and water.

I feel farthest from Iñigo when he seems to ignore his needs and inflict miseries upon himself. A healthy discipline, chastity, and solidarity with the poor are all honorable desires, of course, but so often Iñigo seems to go over the top, to hate and scourge what is wholly natural and, in essence, pure gift. God finds us where we are, however, and God found Iñigo with one foot in the Middle Ages, believing, as the faithful did then, that the flesh and spirit were at war and fearing that pleasure was a kind of death to the holy. There was little integration of flesh and spirit then, only rivalry and argument. We have not completely shaken those notions to this day.

After two years in Barcelona, his Latin tutor gave Iñigo permission to go to the University of Alcalá, just east of Madrid, where he studied the physics of Albertus Magnus, the logic of Domingo de Soto, and Peter Lombard's twelfth-century theological treatise *Four Books of Sentences*. And in his free time, he said, "he was busy giving spiritual exercises and teaching Christian doctrine and in so doing brought forth fruit for the glory of God."

In so doing he also brought forth the fruit of the Spanish Inquisition, as officials accused Iñigo and his followers of being heretical *Alumbrados*, or Illuminists, because they wore ankle-length cassocks of cheap *pardillo* that looked like religious habits and because Iñigo was giving high-tension religious instruction whose affect often produced fainting and weeping in his audiences. In Holy Week of the year 1527, Iñigo was jailed, and held in a cell for forty-two days, but he frustrated officials with his frankness and serenity, and depositions from his female admirers only proved how orthodox were his principles: "Weekly confession and Communion, examination of conscience twice a day, the practice of meditation according to the three powers of the soul," that is, memory, intellect, and will. When Iñigo was finally released in June, he was given as a kind of peace offering a free black cassock and biretta, the fashion for students then, and was forbidden to teach on faith and morals until he completed four years of theology.

For that he went to the prestigious University of Salamanca, but within a fortnight he was dining with Dominican friars who heard hints of the Dutch humanism of Desiderius Erasmus in his talk and held him in their chapel until an inquisitor from Toledo could get there. Iñigo was again jailed. After twenty-two days of being shackled to a post in a foul upper room, he was interrogated by four judges, who found no great error in his teaching and ruled that he could catechize again, but only insofar as he did not try to define what were mortal and what were venial sins. Ethical distinctions in conscience and conduct were so at the heart of his public talks that Iñigo may have felt that they'd told him to teach geometry without azimuths. Hamstrung by that sentence, he thought it was high time to get out of Spain.

After hiking seven hundred miles north, he arrived in Paris on February 2, 1528, and went to the Sorbonne, a consortium of fifty colleges that was the greatest international center of learning in Europe. Even in peculiar times, he was a peculiar student, a frail mystic who knew no French, was less than fluent in Latin, and was then in his thirty-seventh year. Because his hasty studies at Barcelona and Alcalá had left him deficient in fundamentals, Iñigo enrolled in humanities at the Collège de Montaigu and studied Latin with boys of nine and ten. Habitually heedless of money, he asked a Spanish friend at Montaigu to hold for safekeeping the princely sum he had been given for his education, but the friend frittered it away on wild living, and by Easter Iñigo was forced to find horrible lodging far away at the hospice of Saint-Jacques and to go begging again, first among the wealthy Spanish merchants in Bruges and Antwerp in Flanders, and finally in England, garnering enough that he himself was able to be a magnanimous almsgiver back in France.

In the fall of 1529, Iñigo transferred to the Collège de Sainte

Barbe, home mainly to the Portuguese at the University of Paris, and shared housing with his professor and with two highly regarded scholars whose lives he was to significantly change. The first was Pierre Favre of Savoy, a gentle, intelligent, psychologically intuitive twenty-three-year-old whose intent was the Catholic priesthood and who'd recently passed examinations for the licentiate in philosophy. Francisco de Javier—or Francis Xavier, as we know him—was also twenty-three, and a handsome, jubilant, outgoing grandee and fellow Basque from Navarre who wanted to be a famous professor or counselor to princes, as his father had been, and was already a regent in philosophy in the Collège de Beauvais. Each finally succumbed to Iñigo's imprecations and agreed to go through a full month of his Spiritual Exercises. Upon finishing them, Favre and Xavier were inflamed "friends in the Lord" with Iñigo, filling their hours with theological studies, religious practices and conversations, and in thinking about a future that still had no firm goal. Allied with them were the Portuguese student Simão Rodrigues, who was at Sainte Barbe on a royal burse from King John III; Diego Laínez and Alfonso Salmerón, both Spaniards and former students at Alcalá; and Nicolás de Bobadilla, a philosopher at Alcalá and theologian at Valladolid before becoming a regent in the Collège de Calvi.

Ignatius de Loyola was given the title Master of Arts at Easter ceremonies in 1534. We have no certainty about his change of name. It may be that he thought of the familiar name Ignacio as a easier variant of Iñigo, but it's also possible that in the age of reformation he was inspired by the Syrian prelate, Ignatius of Antioch, who faced the persecutions and theological disputes of second-century Christianity and whom Emperor Trajan threw to the lions in Rome.

We do know that Ignatius was seeking priesthood by Easter of 1534, and in preparation for holy orders he was studying the *Summa Theologica* of Thomas Aquinas with the highly esteemed Dominican faculty of the Collège de Saint-Jacques. But Pierre Favre was the first companion ordained, and on August 15, 1534, the feast of the Assumption of Mary, he celebrated Mass for his friends on the heights of Montmartre in the shrine of the martyrdom of Saint Denis and his companions. At Communion, Ignatius, Xavier, Rodrigues, Laínez, Salmerón, and Bobadilla professed vows to a life of poverty and to undertake a pilgrimage to Jerusalem or, failing that, to offer themselves to the Vicar of Christ, the pope, for whatever mission he wished. Chastity was not vowed but presumed, for they all intended to receive holy orders. Even Ignatius seems not to have thought that their profession was the origin of a new religious order, but in hindsight it was.

Within a year, Claude Le Jay, a Savoyard friend of Pierre Favre, had completed the Spiritual Exercises and made the same vows, and a year after that, again on August 15, the group was increased by Paschase Broet of Picardy and Jean Codure of Dauphiné. Ignatius missed those ceremonies. Chronic stomach pains that were prompted by gallstones forced him in 1535 to go on horseback to Azpeitia for the familiar weather and air of home that was thought then to heal a host of ills. After some health-restoring time in Spain, he went ahead of his "friends in the Lord" to Venice where they all hoped to find a ship to the Holy Land. While waiting for them to get there, Ignatius studied theology, taught catechism, and helped a Spanish priest named Diego Hoces through the Spiritual Exercises and later welcomed him as another companion. And, it would seem, Ignatius was thinking a good deal about how a religious foundation ought to be organized, for he wrote a chiding letter to Gian Pietro Caraffa, a founder of the first order of clerks regular, called the Theatines:

> When a man of rank and exalted dignity wears a habit more ornate and lives in a room better furnished than the other religious of his order, I am neither scandalized nor disedified. However, it would do well to consider how the saints have conducted themselves, St. Dominic and St. Francis, for example; and it would be good to have recourse to light from on high; for, after all, a thing may be licit without being expedient.

Of the Theatines in Venice, who shut themselves in their houses of prayer and passively filled their needs with gifts from the faithful, Ignatius wrote that people "will say that they do not see the purpose of this Order; and that the saints, without failing in confidence in God, acted otherwise."

Caraffa, the Italian bishop of Chieti, was a good but impatient and tempestuous Neapolitan who in December would be created a cardinal, and he did not take kindly to faultfinding from a Spaniard, an unfinished theologian, and a forty-five-year-old mendicant who was not yet even a priest. We have lost his reply to Ignatius, but we know the hostility of Caraffa was such that when the companions from the Sorbonne finally got to Italy in 1537, Ignatius sent them on to Rome without him so that Cardinal Caraffa would have no punitive reason to foil their Easter presentation to Pope Paul III.

At that papal audience in Castel Sant' Angelo, the humble but impressive companions told the pope of their project to go to Jerusalem and begin an apostolate to the infidel there, and of their further wish to receive holy orders. Knowing the Turkish fleet was belligerently plying the Mediterranean, Paul III quietly put it that, "I do not think you will reach Jerusalem." And yet their requests were not only granted by the pontiff, but they were given close to three hundred *escudos* for the voyage.

In Venice on the feast of Saint John the Baptist, June 24, 1537, Vincenzo Nigusanti, bishop of Arbe, ordained Ignatius, Bobadilla, Codure, Xavier, Laínez, and Rodrigues under the title of poverty, *ad titulum paupertatis*. Bishop Nigusanti would later frequently repeat that he'd never gotten such pure consolation from an ordination. In humility, Ignatius put off presiding at his first Mass for a year and a half, so he would be the last of the ten to have that honor, and so he could perhaps celebrate it at a shrine in Bethlehem. When that proved impossible, he chose to celebrate his first Mass in Rome on Christmas 1538 at the church of Santa Maria Maggiore, which Christians believed held the true crib of the child Jesus—a worthy substitute, he thought, for Christ's birthplace.

While waiting for a ship to Palestine in the fall of 1537, the new priests preached in the streets and performed works of mercy in hospitals throughout the Republic of Venice, but for the first time in nearly forty years however, hot rumors of war and piracy kept any ship from sailing to the East. Gathering together again in Vicenza that winter, the priests chose to be patient in their hopes of sea passage and to concentrate their preaching in cities with universities, where they might find high-minded students to join them. If anyone asked who they were, they agreed, "it seemed to them most fitting that they should take the name of him whom they had as their head, by calling themselves the 'company of Jesus.'"

Acknowledging at last that their hoped-for pilgrimage to Jerusalem was improbable, Ignatius, Favre, and Laínez walked two hundred fifty miles south to Rome in order to offer their services to the pope in fulfillment of the vow they had professed on Montmartre. Stopping in the outskirts of Rome, at a place called La Storta, Ignatius and Laínez went into a chapel, where Ignatius prayed that Mary hold him in her heart as she did her son. Then he felt a change in his soul, and later told Laínez that he beheld "Christ with the cross on his shoulder, and next to Him the eternal Father, who said to Him: 'I want you to take this man as your servant,' and Jesus thus took him and said: 'I want you to serve us.'" Ignatius also told Laínez "that it seemed to him as if God the Father had imprinted the following words in his heart: *Ego ero vobis Romae propitius*." I will be favorable to you in Rome.

Uplifted by the La Storta illumination, Ignatius and his friends went into the city in late November 1537, and were again graciously received by the pontiff. Hearing their offer of service, Paul III gladly assigned Diego Laínez to teach scholastic theology at La Sapienza, a palace that housed the University of Rome. Pierre Favre was to fill an office in positive theology there, giving commentaries on Sacred Scripture. With those surprising first papal assignments, the Italian Compagnia di Gesù ever so gradually became a company of teachers, but Ignatius sought to forgo the classroom in favor of giving the Spiritual Exercises in Rome, first to the ambassador of Emperor Charles V, then to the president of the pontifical commission for reform of the Church, to the ambassador of Siena, to a Spanish physician, and to Francesco de Estrada, a Spanish priest who'd worked for the formidable Cardinal Caraffa in Rome and been fired. Upon completion of the Exercises, Estrada too joined the Company of Jesus, and late in life would be named the Jesuit provincial of Aragón in Spain.

Rome became Ignatius's and the companions' Jerusalem. After Easter 1538, all of them gathered there and, through the skills of Pietro Codacio, a papal chamberlain and the first Italian companion, got title to the Church of Santa Maria della Strada, Our Lady of the Wayside, chosen by Ignatius because it was on a high-traffic piazza that was handily near the papal court, government offices, a significant Jewish community, palaces of the upper class, houses of prostitutes, and the hovels of the poor. Santa Maria della Strada was the first foundation in the Eternal City for a host of what Ignatius called "works of piety": homes for children that were supported by the Confraternity of Saint Mary of the Visitation of Orphans; the Catechumens, a house for the religious instruction of new Jewish converts; the Casa Santa Marta, a house of refuge for former prostitutes; and the Conservatorio delle Vergini Miserabili, a house for girls who might be attracted to prostitution. Significant to their primary ministry later was their work at the Collegio Romano, a high school in grammar, humanities, and Christian doctrine that was free for boys in Rome. Costs of education were defrayed by a magnificent gift from Francisco Borgia, the duke of Gandía in Spain, the great-grandson of Pope Alexander VI and King Ferdinand V, a father of eight, and, after the death of his wife, a Jesuit priest and the third superior general.

But the foundation of the greatest importance was, of course, that of the Society of Jesus—*societas* being the Latin for company—which was confirmed by Paul III in the papal bull *Regimini Militantis Ecclesiae* on September 27, 1540. Ignatius sketched the "formula" for the institute in five brief chapters that he introduced in this way:

> **Whoever desires to serve as a soldier of God beneath the banner of the cross in our Society, which we desire to be designated by the name of Jesus, and in it to serve the Lord**

> **alone and his vicar on earth, should, after a solemn vow of chastity, keep what follows in mind. He is a member of a community founded chiefly to strive for the progress of souls in Christian life and doctrine, and for the propagation of the faith by means of the ministry of the word, the Spiritual Exercises, and works of charity . . .**

Upon hearing the "formula" read to him, the aged Paul III had orally given his approval and added, "*Digitus Dei est hic*," "The finger of God is here." Ignatius and Jean Codure later expanded "A First Sketch of the Institute of the Society of Jesus" into *Constitutions* of forty-nine points regulating frugality, governance, admission and formation of novices, and housing and other practical matters, but generally offering Jesuits flexibility in their ways of proceeding in order to give room to, as Ignatius put it, "the internal guidance of the Holy Spirit."

In fulfillment of their rules on governance, on April 8, 1541, Ignatius was elected the first superior general of the Society of Jesus, the only ballot against him being his own. Xavier's ballot was probably typical of the others; he voted for "our old leader and true father, Don Ignacio, who, since he brought us together with no little effort, will also with similar effort know how to preserve, govern, and help us advance from good to better."

Ignatius was then fifty and far different from the man he'd fantasized he'd be when he was a page to Spanish royalty, or a pilgrim to the Holy Land, or a philosopher at the Sorbonne. Ever seeking the greater glory of God and the good of souls,

Ignatius surely imagined a grander fate than that of fifteen years of grinding office and managerial work in the house for forty professed fathers that he built on Via Aracoeli, or that of having as one of his prime contributions to history his hand-cramping composition of more than seven thousand letters to his scattered Jesuit sons—twelve full volumes in the *Monumenta Historica Societatis Iesu.* We hear no regret in his letters, however, no aching to be elsewhere, only geniality and hunger for news as he writes to the Jesuit *periti* at the Council of Trent; gentle hints as to how a homosexual scholastic could preserve his chastity; tenderness for the many Spanish women for whom he was a spiritual director; sympathy for a priest in Sicily afflicted by scruples, as he had been; fatherly reproof as he orders a house in Portugal to curb their hard penances; affection to his dearest friend Xavier in Japan: "We have rejoiced in the Lord that you have arrived with health and that doors have opened to have the Gospel preached in that region."

His holiness was unmistakeable; he practiced self-mastery until there seemed to be no difference between God's will and his own. "*Eres en tu casa,*" was his wide-armed greeting to anyone who visited him—"You are at home"—and all who talked with him left with the impression that he was kindliness itself: Michelangelo was so affected by Ignatius that he offered to build the Church of the Gesù for nothing. Ever a mystic, at times the saint was in the midst of an official transaction when his thoughts would lift up to God and hang there, and his witnesses would shyly shuffle their shoes until he got back to his papers again. But there were also stories of him surprising a melancholic with a jig in order to cheer him up, and his happiness was such that he said he could no longer apply his own rules for discernment of spirits because he was finding consolation in all things—he once said he saw the Holy Trinity in the leaf of an orange tree. Although children threw apples at him when he first preached in the streets of Rome—probably because of his horrid Italian—he soon was as genuinely beloved as the pope. In fact, he was so highly thought of by prelates that in the 1550 conclave at which Julius III was elected pontiff, Ignatius de Loyola received five votes. And we can get a feeling for the high esteem in which he was held by his fellow Jesuits when we read letters such as this from a Frans de Costere, S.J., of Cologne:

> The day before yesterday I saw for the first time, with indescribable joy and eagerness, Reverend Father Ignatius. I could not see enough of him. For his countenance is such that one cannot look upon it long enough. The old man was walking in the garden, leaning on a cane. His face shone with godliness. He is mild, friendly, and amiable so that he speaks with the learned and the unlearned, with important people and little people, all in the same way: a man worthy of all praise and reverence. No one can deny that a great reward is prepared for him in heaven . . . .

But Gian Pietro Caraffa, whom Ignatius insulted in his frank letter about the Theatines, thought of him as a tyrant and a false idol. In fact, the friction between Caraffa and Ignatius was such that when, in 1555, Ignatius heard that Caraffa had been elected pontiff, as Paul IV, Ignatius's face went white, and he falteringly limped into a chapel to pray. But after a while he appeared again and happily said the new Pope Paul IV would be good to them, which he was but only to a degree, for after Ignatius died he tried to merge his Theatines with the Jesuits, and briefly forced them to sing the Divine Office in choir and to limit the superior general's term to three years.

Even some of his first companions had difficulties with Ignatius, though: Nicolás de Bobadilla angrily called him "a rascally sophist and a Basque spoiled by flattery" and Simão Rodrigues, whose contrariness prompted Ignatius to recall him from Portugal, claimed that the superior general did so out of passion and hate, and with slight regard for his reputation. Juan de Polanco was supposed to have made do with hardly one compliment during his nine years as Ignatius's secretary; Jerónimo Nadal was often so harshly criticized that he couldn't hold back his tears; and Diego Laínez, a favorite of his, once objected, "What have I done against the Society that this saint treats me this way?"

An affectionate man who was wary of his *affectus*, Ignatius was probably hard on his friends in accordance with his fundamental principle of *agere contra*, that is, to go against or contradict one's own inclinations if they are not for the honor and glory of God or for the good of others. We see hints of this in the sixteenth annotation to his *Spiritual Exercises*, in which Ignatius wrote: "If by chance the exercitant feels an affection or inclination to something in a disordered way, it is profitable for that person to strive with all possible effort to come over to the opposite of that to which he or she is wrongly attached."

He was harder on himself than on his friends, punishing himself for his sins, getting to bed late and waking up at half past four, hardly ever going outside the house or strolling in the gardens, which he insisted on for his "sons," dining on food that he called a penance, holding his gaze on the ground when he did walk in Rome, loving plainchant but forbidding choir for the order.

All of that took its toll. By 1556 his health was failing to such an extent that to his chronic stomach pains were added a hardening of the liver, high fevers, and general exhaustion. He was rarely seen outside his room and ate little more than fish scraps and broths and lettuce prepared with oil. Spells of illness had troubled him so frequently in the past, however, and he'd shown such resilience in healing, that no one was especially upset by his confinement, and physicians often failed even to visit him as they ministered to others in the house who were thought to be far worse off, among them his friend Diego Laínez. But Ignatius knew how far he'd sunk and on the afternoon of July 30, he thought it would be fitting if Juan de Polanco, the secretary of the Society, would go and inform Paul IV that Ignatius "was near the end and almost without hope of temporal life, and that he humbly begged from His Holiness his blessing for himself and for Master Laínez, who was also in danger." Misprizing his superior's condition, Polanco asked if he could put off the walk, because he was trying to finish some letters for Spain before a ship sailed. Ignatius told him, "The sooner you go, the more satisfied I shall be; however, do as you wish."

Brother Tommaso Cannicari, the infirmarian, slept in a cell next to the superior general's quarters, and off and on heard Ignatius praying until, after midnight, he heard only, over and over again, the Spanish sigh, "*Ay, Dios!*" At sunrise the fathers in the house saw that Ignatius was dying, and Cannicari hurried to find the superior general's confessor while Polanco hurried to the papal residence to request the Holy Father's blessing. But it was too late. Two hours after sunrise on Friday morning, July 31, 1556, Ignatius of Loyola died, without having received the quite unnecessary graces of extreme unction or viaticum or papal blessing.

In the first week of the *Spiritual Exercises*, Ignatius had offered this as the "Principle and Foundation" for all the meditations that would follow:

> Human beings are created to praise, reverence, and serve God our Lord, and by means of doing this to save their souls.
>
> The other things on the face of the earth are created for the human beings, to help them in the pursuit of the end for which they are created.
>
> From this it follows that we ought to use these things to

> the extent that they help us toward our end, and free ourselves from them to the extent that they hinder us from it.
>
> To attain this it is necessary to make ourselves indifferent to all created things, in regard to everything which is left to our free will and is not forbidden. Consequently, on our own part we ought not to seek health rather than sickness, wealth rather than poverty, honor rather than dishonor, a long life rather than a short one, and so on in all other matters.
>
> Rather, we ought to desire and choose only that which is more conducive to the end for which we are created.

Saint Irenaeus said that the glory of God is a human being fully alive. But what is it to be fully alive? We are apt to look at Ignatius's life as one of harsh discipline and privation, and find only loss in his giving up of family, inheritance, financial security, prestige, luxury, sexual pleasure. But he looked at his life as an offering to the God he called *liberalidad*, freedom, and God blessed that gift a hundredfold in the Society of Jesus. The house of Loyola ended when Doña Magdalena de Loyola y Borgia died childless in 1626, but in that same year there were 15,535 Jesuits in 36 provinces, with 56 seminaries, 44 novitiates, 254 houses, and 443 colleges in Europe and the Baltic States, Japan, India, Macao, the Philippines, and the Americas.

The Story of Cain

In Congregation, *an anthology of essays on the Bible edited by David Rosenberg, Isaac Bashevis Singer wrote: "I am still learning the art of writing from the Book of Genesis." A few years later David Rosenberg, the acclaimed translator of* The Book of J, *quoted Singer in his invitation to me and nineteen other novelists, poets, dramatists, and essayists to comment on the familiar stories of Genesis from a writer's perspective. Enormous latitude was given to our investigations. We were urged, for example, to consider a story's various renditions in other literature over the centuries, or to talk about its influence in our own work. In our phone conversation, David asked if I had a particular story in mind, and my response was immediate: "I'll do Cain and Abel."*

The Story of Cain

Rob and I were Boy Scouts in Omaha, Nebraska. And it was time to vote for patrol leader, the highest-ranking officer in

Troop Sixteen. We may have been twelve then. We were still called The Twins. I have forgotten the formalities of the voting, only that it was held in secret, and the tallying behind closed doors took far longer than it should have. I have forgotten even who won an election that seemed hugely important to me then. What I recall is that a boy other than me was chosen, and I was shocked. Seeing my face, a friend who'd been in on the tally confided that I had in fact won the election, but the scoutmaster thought it would hurt my brother's feelings if I was favored over him.

Walking home with Rob that night I fumed for a few blocks and then shouted in fury, "It's always going to be this way! You're always going to hold me back!"

Rob, I remember, looked stricken.

Rob is always Abel in my memories. I am always Cain.

Even as far back as infancy it was that way. One afternoon Rob was put in his crib and I in mine, and my mother tried to tiptoe to the door. But I must have been hungry for affection or some further sign of my uniqueness, for as Rob fell asleep, I got up on my knees and held onto the crib slats and shook my head from side to side, saying, "No, no, no, no!" And she thought that so charmingly honest a need that she held me for a few minutes more.

Envy and rivalry. We were paging through magazines on one of those hot and endless August afternoons of childhood when Rob got the notion to try to imitate a photograph of the glamorous, silken spread of Skippy peanut butter on a pristine slice of white bread. I heard him working in the kitchen for too many minutes, and then he proudly strolled back with his honed and sculpted peanut butter creation in his hand.

"Look," he said. "It's perfect!"

And it was. Even art of a kind. But, alas, the temptation was just too strong. I whacked his hand upwards so that the peanut butter swocked into his face. Rob was, one could say, dismayed.

"You know, it's funny," my brother said, when I read these pages to him, "but in *my* memories you're always Cain, too."

The feel is that of a fairy tale. The firstborn of the first man and woman was a son, Kayin; and he was followed by another son, Hevel. Kayin grew up to be a farmer, while Hevel herded sheep, and it was their habit at harvest time to offer a sacrifice to God of the first fruits of the fields and the firstlings of the flock, for it was God whose gifts they were. But Kayin grew hard of heart and put on the high altar only the fruits and grains that had fallen on the ground. Was God blind that he couldn't tell the difference? God found fault with Kayin, but favored Hevel, and Kayin fought with his brother over that, and he killed him. Then God asked Kayin, though he knew, where his brother was, and Kayin tried to pretend he had no idea. And God's wrath was great, for he'd heard Kayin's brother's blood crying out from the reddened ground, and God damned Kayin for his murder, and damned his tilling of the soil, forcing him to wander the earth, far from the face of God.

• • •

Chapter 4:1–16 of the book of Genesis follows up the fall from paradise with an analogical tale in which a second generation is offered the choice of obedience or estrangement, of heeding God's warnings or facing death. With the Cain and Abel narrative we get the first mention of sin and the first statement of the important themes of family conflict and competition that permeate this book of begettings. If the story was adapted, as some propose, from an older folktale about the hostilities among shepherds and farmers, the correspondence between source and finished text is no doubt as far distant as that between Holinshed's *Chronicles* and Shakespeare's *Macbeth*. For the raw power and wisdom and psychological complexity in this fable are wholly lacking in other ancient texts, where the focus was on a pantheon of glamorous gods, and flesh-and-blood humanity was thought to be an unworthy subject for writerly expression. In fact, reading contemporaneous texts only heightens the awe one feels for the economy, sophistication, and primal force of this book of genius.

We feel the far-ranging influence of Cain and Abel throughout the Hebrew Bible; in the Gospel narratives of Jesus, the good shepherd, and Judas, his betrayer; and further on in the Old English Mystery plays that were performed on high holy days such as Whitsuntide or the feast of Corpus Christi. The fall from paradise was, of course, a popular theme among slogging farmers and trade unionists who wanted particular someones to blame for their hard lot. And no one was more villainous than Cayn, or Cayme, a rough and raffish peasant much like themselves, but avaricious and arrogant, too, like the lords and high-and-mighties in the cities. Often Cain withheld his finest produce out of spite for his misfortunes, offering God the fallen corn on the ground on the principle that if Cain and his family were forced to eat that, it ought to be good enough for His Highness. Abel fulfilled the function of village priest in the Mysteries, worshiping and thanking God with an offering of the finest of his flock. While Cain is hot-tempered, insolent, and sullen, Abel is all piety and rectitude, too good to be true, even a bit of a simp; a hand raised against him seems oddly fitting, and there must have been more than a few in the audiences who felt a forbidden pleasure at seeing him laid out.

Lord Byron interestingly altered the old tradition with *Cain,* an ill-received psychological drama in which the first murderer is an aspiring and proud intellectual whose high estimate of himself is sundered when, on a journey into space and the past, Lucifer offers him an illustration of his own paltriness in comparison with infinite things. Abased, brooding, and despondent, Cain finds in Abel's bloody sacrifice a shame to creation, and in heedless fury at a Creator who has burdened humanity with frailty and inadequacies, Cain strikes down his brother with an iron. His blood flowing into the ground, Abel has time for one last prayer: that his own soul be received into Heaven and that

Cain be forgiven "for he knew not what he did." Looking about him, as though jolted from a sleep, Cain asks, "Where am I? Alone! Where's Abel? Where's Cain? Can it be that I am he? My brother, awake! Why liest thou so on the green earth? 'Tis not the hour of slumber." Cain's crime is not one of villainy or malice, but of rebellion and mischance, and when he finds out what he's done, he's filled with remorse. We do not suffer with him, however. We can do little more than sigh.

Each of these later renditions is hobbled by the character of Abel. The first victim of the first murder is perhaps a man to pity, but we feel no ache at his loss. Abel slides off the page like a bookmark, a symbol of what we ought to be, a fine abstraction, like righteousness, that we agree our friends should pursue with far greater diligence. We have learned, since the Book of Genesis, that a good plot requires worthy opponents, a fitting antagonist to the protagonist, such as Peter Shaffer offers us in *Amadeus.*

There Cain is Antonio Salieri, an Italian composer in the Viennese court and a former teacher of Ludwig van Beethoven, who has discovered, after forty-one operas, a requiem mass, and a surfeit of sacred music, that his work is dull and mediocre, wholly lacking in passion. The focus of his education is Wolfgang Amadeus Mozart, for Salieri hears him play on the piano his Serenade for 13 Wind Instruments and is shaken by the absolute beauty of the piece. At their next meeting, when Salieri welcomes Herr Mozart to the Viennese court with his own rather pedestrian march, Mozart is fascinated by the wrong turns Salieri's composition took and with a few effortless flourishes transforms it into a masterpiece. And Salieri finds himself thinking of murder, not out of hatred for Mozart, but for God, who unfairly has lavished such talent and virtuosity on a conceited, spiteful, infantile "creature" while withholding it from him.

My own variation on the fable of Cain and his brother was played out in my historical novel *The Assassination of Jesse James by the Coward Robert Ford*. I found in my research that Bob Ford had been obsessed by the James gang ever since he was a boy, frequently imagining himself as one of them, but also thinking of the fame he would garner if he were to capture one of the outlaws. His chance came when he and his brother Charley insinuated themselves as friends of Jesse during his and his brother Frank's final train robbery, in Blue Cut, Missouri.

The James gang fell apart after that hold-up, as one man after the next was either killed or jailed. Ever watchful, even paranoid, Jesse James for some reason failed to suspect that Bob Ford was conspiring with the government to arrest or assassinate him. But perhaps Jesse intended to kill the Ford brothers himself when he invited them to the house on a hill in St. Joseph, Missouri, where he was hiding with his wife and two children under the alias of Thomas Howard. Quite possibly he was simply mistaken about the Ford brothers' seeming friendship, and what Jesse interpreted as hero worship and flattery and imitation were in fact the scheming and dissembling of petty thieves. Bob Ford finally did not so much want to be *like* Jesse James, as he thought in his youth, but wanted rather to *be* him. The factual human being was getting in the way of his own fabulous dreams of himself. And so he betrayed his friend by firing his gun into the back of his head as Jesse frittered about in his house one April morning in a kind of cat-and-mouse game. Hearing the gunfire, Zerelda James ran out of the kitchen and fell on her knees by her husband, who was lying slain on the floor. She looked up at the Ford brothers and asked Bob, much as God asked Cain, "What have you done?" And, like Cain, Bob tried to shirk culpability for his crime, saying the gun went off accidentally.

Bob was treated as a hero for a short time after the shooting, but was given only a portion of the financial reward he sought and was forced to find an income through theatrical reenactments of his crime. Each night, in faraway towns, his brother Charley would have a blank fired at his head as lamely he portrayed the famous killer who was himself killed. Each night Bob Ford would tell the audience, without shame or remorse, just how he did what he did. As time went on, Charley could not handle the hatred they increasingly felt from the crowds, and within a few vears he committed suicide. But Bob haughtily continued, like Cain a fugitive and vagabond on the earth, until he fetched up in Creede, Colorado, where he owned a tavern and where one night he was killed by a shotgun blast from a drunken man named Ed O'Kelly who claimed he did it to avenge his fallen idol. Blood will have blood.

• • •

In the King James Version of the Bible, the Lord warns Cain, "If thou doest well, shalt thou not be accepted? and if thou doest not well, sin lieth at the door. And unto thee shall be his desire, and thou shalt rule over him." And in the next sentence, "it came to pass, when they were in the field, that Cain rose up against Abel his brother, and slew him."

I find it a chilling story, even in its fleeting telling, even with so much left out. We so often find ourselves ruled by sin that the fate of Cain seems not far off at all. I have, for example, one more memory. Rob and I were teenagers, and in the kitchen one night. He washed the dishes; I dried them. We weren't arguing. But as we goofed off I flipped the dish towel over his head and astonished him by roughly tightening it at his neck and holding it taut. Was there hostility in it? I felt no emotion, only a kind of fierce energy and fascination—*Look what I can do.* And then he fell to his knees and onto his back. His face was white as I knelt over him. Life seemed to be leaking onto the floor. Was murder that easy? Right then I was thinking I was going to be in big trouble if our folks found out I'd killed him. You just don't do that sort of thing. Slapping his cold cheeks like they do in movies, and hushing my voice in order to keep my heinous crime hidden for a little longer, I whispered, "Wake up! Please, Rob! Please don't die!"

Rob opened his eyes in bland surprise and sheepishly looked at me. "What happened?"

With huge relief I sat back on my heels and got into a change of character. "You fainted," I told him, and helped him to his feet. We finished washing the dishes in silence, as if nothing had happened, and I heard the television on in the living room, and the shrieks of a sitcom audience, and the soft easy laughter of my parents.

Affliction and Grace: Religious Experience in the Poetry of Gerard Manley Hopkins

I first encountered the poetry of Gerard Manley Hopkins in a high school anthology at Creighton Preparatory School in Omaha. I was sixteen, the instructor was probably twenty-six, and neither one of us had the foggiest idea of what "The Windhover" was all about, we just knew it was full of hard words and peculiar stress marks. I was not immediately a fan.

I did, however, fall madly in love with the poetry of Dylan Thomas. I purchased his Collected Poems *with money I earned as a greenskeeper for the Omaha Parks & Recreation Department, and was sorely put out when I heard that Robert Lowell had said Dylan Thomas was the author of five good poems and no one knew which ones they were. I did, and there were far more than five.*

About one-eighth of my bloodline is Welsh, so I fabricated a jocular friendship for the word-drunk Welshman, and since I was then feeling quite a lot like "a windy boy and a bit and the black spit of the chapel fold," Dylan Thomas was my flamboyant hero. I even executed a fairly good pen-and-ink portrait of him that hung over my bed. I have no idea where it came from, but Constantine Fitzgibbon's biography of Dylan Thomas found its way into my family's library, which was then primarily Reader's Digest Condensed Books, and I found myself, in the funk of being eighteen, wholly absorbed in the young Dylan's wild and reckless life, wanting to flare and blaze as he did, deciding that his wife's name, Caitlin, was probably the most beautiful on earth, and discovering that one of Dylan Thomas's foremost influences was the Reverend Gerard Manley Hopkins, S.J.

My fascination with Thomas forced me to give Hopkins another try in college, and I felt an affinity I hadn't in high school. Difficulty was no longer so off-putting for one thing, his Ignatian theology was no longer something I was ignorant of, the chromatic concreteness of his imagery was just what I was trying to add to my prose, and I was newly enlisted in the cult of those who find delight in etymologies and woefully little-used words. Wanwood, sillion, cumber, throstle. I had trouble fitting them into conversations, and yet my life was richer for hearing them.

We considered five of Hopkins's poems in the freshman English survey at Creighton University, and only one, "The Windhover," in my senior year course in Modern British and American Poetry. But Hopkins was present enough in my consciousness that when I felt affronted by one of my peers in my junior year I recall writing: "Wert thou my enemy, O thou my friend, how wouldst thou worse, I wonder, than thou dost defeat, thwart me?" The friend never answered, but stayed far away for a while.

At lunch with a Jesuit friend a few years ago, I was approached by Paul Locatelli, S.J., the president of Santa Clara University, who said,

"I have an offer you can't refuse." We had dinner and he described a professorship in creative writing that would be funded with an endowed chair. An attractive offer, but I was gainfully employed elsewhere and wasn't sure I ought to change jobs, so I secretly prayed to Father Hopkins about whether I ought to take it or not. The next night I got a call from Father Locatelli asking for my decision about the job, and adding, "We'll call it the Gerard Manley Hopkins chair. Does that mean anything to you?" It did. And I imagined Gerard in heaven, smiling.

Other poets have been important to me—W. B. Yeats, Wallace Stevens, Sylvia Plath, Elizabeth Bishop, John Berryman—but Hopkins has remained my favorite because he, like T. S. Eliot, is not so easily solved. Any interpretation insists on further interpretation. An infinite number of layers seems available for peeling.

What Hopkins did extraordinarily well is imitate in poetry the operations of the mind and spirit at a heightened moment of graced perception. We have all had the experience of a song or a photograph igniting an explosion of tangential feelings and memories that we struggle to contain. Whether through psychological acuity or sheer force and clarity of intellect, Hopkins could find the unifying factor among wildly differing things, and rejoice in their being fathered-forth by God.

Concentrating solely on the poetry, however, is in some way to miss the point, for Gerard Manley Hopkins, the man, seems to me as inspiring as his work. Who among our finest poets has lived as sane and honorable a life? Contrary, kind, opinionated, humorous, prone to depression, ill-at-ease in public, fond of puns, jealous, Hopkins was nevertheless an English gentleman and the opposite of dissolute: an abstemious, disciplined, hardworking teacher, a wise and meditative homilist, an affectionate son and brother and friend, a good priest. Even his most quarrelsome biographers portray a life of fidelity, integrity, and service, with a Christ-like devotion to his calling. He was a gift to our time, if not to his own. Praise him.

AFFLICTION AND GRACE: RELIGIOUS EXPERIENCE IN THE POETRY OF GERARD MANLEY HOPKINS

In his handbook on Christian spirituality, *When the Well Runs Dry,* the Jesuit priest Thomas H. Green compares the patterns of growth in prayer to those of human romance and marriage. We are attracted to God at first as fascinated strangers. We make a tentative approach and are thrilled to feel God's tender response. Affection deepens to infatuation as our spiritual conversations continue and we become obsessed in getting to know the Lord. We read and meditate and use affective imagery to picture this alluring Other. We have said yes to God and are engaged, and yet we may still be hesitant and timid. We need to get hooked. Hence, God graces us with a honeymoon of great consolations and a gradual movement from head to heart, from courtship to commitment. Some people do not go beyond this phase, but others are graced with a further stage, one of alienation and languishment and feelings of forlorn separation, even estrangement, a phase that Saint John of the Cross called the dark night of the soul.

The fruits of this affliction are finally quite fulfilling and profound: We are taught to let go, to give up our futile attempts at control and find the persistent love of God even without consolations. We are purified through our suffering, for we frankly encounter ourselves as we truly are and are fully transformed by that revelation. We are taught to desire God for God's sake and through that teaching we move from our heart to our will.

Saint Ignatius of Loyola and Saint Teresa of Ávila both furnish examples of these stages of Christian interior growth in their famous autobiographies, but there is an equally fascinating representation of this hard-wrought religious experience in the poems and so-called terrible sonnets of the English Jesuit, Gerard Manley Hopkins.

1. INFATUATION

Gerard Manley Hopkins, S.J. (1844–1889), was the firstborn of Grace and Manley Hopkins, an Anglican insurance adjuster in Hampstead, England, and consul-general for Hawaii. Gerard was sent to boarding school at Highgate and in 1863 placed into Balliol College at Oxford, where he principally read Latin and Greek. A tremendous devotion to Our Lady, fondness for Anglican High Church ritualism and the philosophy of the fifteenth-century Italian Dominican Girolamo Savonarola, and difficulties with the separation from Rome by King Henry VIII finally convinced him to forsake his hopes of further fellowships at Oxford and be received into the Catholic Church by John

Henry Newman in October 1866. In a letter to a friend, Hopkins wrote:

> My conversion is due to the following reasons mainly (I have put them down without order)—(i) simply and strictly drawn arguments partly my own, partly others', (ii) common sense, (iii) reading the Bible, especially the Holy Gospels, where texts like 'Thou art Peter' (the evasions proposed for this alone are enough to make one a Catholic) and the manifest position of St. Peter among the Apostles so pursued me that at one time I thought it best to stop thinking of them, (iv) an increasing knowledge of the Catholic system (at first under the form of Tractarianism, later in its genuine place), which only wants to be known in order to be loved—its consolations, its marvellous ideal of holiness, the faith and devotion of its children, its multiplicity, its arrays of saints and martyrs, its consistency and unity, its glowing prayers, the daring majesty of its claims, etc etc.

The first poems he wrote at Oxford are full of Christian imagery and themes— "Heaven-Haven," "For a Picture of Saint Dorothea," "Easter Communion," "Myself Unholy"—but they are full, too, of shortfall and wistfulness, of finding himself outside the dwelling place meant for him, as when, in "The Habit of Perfection," he rejects the joys of worldly sensation in favor of a fantasized future of Elected Silence, poverty, and asceticism in religious life and priesthood, where "you shall walk the golden street/ And you unhouse and house the Lord."

Simple conversion to Catholicism was not enough. Even before he graduated from Oxford with a Double First in Latin and Greek, Hopkins was telling friends of his hopes for holy orders, and he seems to have inquired first about joining the Oratorian Congregation and then the Benedictines. But when, in September 1867 at John Henry Newman's Oratory School near Birmingham, he replaced a teacher and fellow convert who left his job to join the Society of Jesus, Hopkins focused his religious feelings on the Jesuits as well and, finding confirmation of his calling in a five-day retreat given by a Jesuit priest who was, significantly, the grandnephew of the poet Samuel Taylor Coleridge, Hopkins soon afterward applied to the Order and finally entered the Novitiate of Manresa House at Roehampton in southwest London in September 1868. Of his decision, he wrote to a friend: "Since I made up my mind to this I have enjoyed the first complete peace of mind I have ever had."

Earlier, in May 1868, he ironically noted in his journal, "Slaughter of the innocents," the only hint he provides of his headstrong and theatrical incineration of his handwritten poetry manuscripts—having sent fair copies of his favorites to his friend, Robert Bridges. In *Hopkins the Jesuit*, Alfred Thomas, S.J., explains:

> We know from what he wrote when he was finally ordained that he thought the dedications of priest and poet were too much alike to exist easily in one person, since they derived from the same sources. And, like Savonarola, he was aware

> that art, even when it was guiltless in itself, could be highly distracting. A vocation to the priesthood implied the renunciation of worldly pursuits, and since poetry was surely dearest of those to him, it was the logical activity to be given up.

2. COMMITMENT

Give up poetry he did, composing only journal entries and letters throughout his two-year novitiate in Roehampton, and only insignificant ceremonial verse throughout his studies in philosophy at Stonyhurst, and his first teaching assignment as a professor of rhetoric at Roehampton. But he was thinking a great deal about poetic form and theory. While at Stonyhurst, he noted in his journal: "What you look hard at seems to look at you, hence the true and false instress of nature." And a few weeks later he wrote:

> This is the time to study inscape in the spraying of trees, for the swelling buds carry them to a pitch which the eye could not else gather—for out of much much more, out of little not much, out of nothing nothing: in these sprays at all events there is a new world of inscape.

Of his famous neologisms—inscape, instress, and sprung rhythm—it is the term inscape that is most telling about his philosophy and his poetic approach, for to Hopkins it was the essential quality or personality of a thing, hinting fractionally at its Creator's perfection, and fully ascertained only through the insight of an onlooker who is in harmony with the being he or she is observing.

This fresh perspective on nature was possibly the fruit of meditations on the *Spiritual Exercises* of Saint Ignatius, especially those having to do with the "Contemplation to Attain the Love of God":

> [The second point is] to look how God dwells in creatures, in the elements giving them being, in the plants vegetating, in the animals feeling in them, in men giving them to understand: and so in me, giving me being, animating me, giving me sensation and making me to understand; likewise making a temple of me, being created to the likeness and image of His Divine Majesty . . .
>
> [The third point is] to consider how God works and labors for me in all things created on the face of the earth—that is, behaves like one who labors—as in the heavens, elements, plants, fruits, cattle, etc., giving them vegetation and sensation, etc.

In August 1874, Hopkins journeyed west to the Theologate at Saint Beuno's College in North Wales, and in September received tonsure and the four minor orders of doorkeepers, readers, exorcists, and acolytes. While he still felt his literary interests had to be subordinate to his religious duties and ideals, Hopkins began to see that his vocation as a poet was equally gracious and sacramental insofar as he communicated to seekers his own profound sense of the immanent presence of Christ in the world.

Writing his friend, Canon Dixon, Hopkins later noted that

> for seven years I wrote nothing but two or three little presentation pieces which occasion called for. But when in the winter of '75 the Deutschland was wrecked in the mouth of the Thames and five Franciscan nuns, exiles from Germany by the Falk Laws, aboard of her were drowned I was affected by the account and happening to say so to my rector he said that he wished someone would write a poem on the subject. On this hint I set to work and, though my hand was out at first, produced one. I had long had haunting my ear the echo of a new rhythm which now I realized on paper.

The London *Times* had reported that a shipwrecked German sister was heard to have cried out in the storm, "O Christ, come quickly." Hopkins's poem was a kind of homily on what she meant by that "perennial cry of Christian faith": that Christ would gather her into a death like his own and through it grant her new life. "The Wreck of the Deutschland" was a difficult, technically innovative, and highly involved ode of two hundred eighty lines that Norman H. Mackenzie, a twentieth-century Hopkins scholar, views as "the most substantial proof that Hopkins was a poet of genius, reforging and re-fusing words as he needed them, and moving well beyond Swinburne in the variety of his living cadences." But neither the Victorian nor the Edwardian age in England was quite ready for Gerard Hopkins. The British Jesuit journal *The Month* at first accepted "The Wreck of the Deutschland" for publication in their August 1876 issue, but finally rejected the poem when Hopkins hesitated at omitting his metrical stresses. And that was the closest he got to a public audience in his lifetime. Nothing of his was published until his friend, Robert Bridges, brought out a hardly noticed collection in 1918. Even in 1927, *The Cambridge Book of Lesser Poets* printed just one poem of his, and that from his Oxford days, "Heaven-Haven"; and it was only in the 1940s, fully one hundred years after his birth, that Gerard Hopkins began to be seen as the giant figure in English literature that he is.

His priestly ordination at St. Beuno's College in September 1877, was the high point for him in a year that was also an annus mirabilis for the unforeseen brilliance of his sudden poetic achievement. "The world is charged wíth the grándeur of God," he wrote in one sonnet. "It will flame out, like shining from shook foil;/ It gathers to a greatness, like the ooze of oil/ Crushed." So it was with his poetry, flaming out from dormancy in fresh and surprising imagery and intricacy of form. "God's Grandeur" takes as its premise the frank, romantic, and sublime presence of the Divinity before the Fall of humankind, and of the hiddenness of that majesty ever since, finding occasional display only in inscapes, here called "the dearest freshness deep down things."

The formal requirements of the sonnet—fourteen lines in iambic pentameter, with the octave composing a theme or sentiment, and the sestet presenting a commentary on it—were successfully meshed with the meditative patterning of the *Spiritual Exercises* in a great many of his poems, "God's Grandeur" being just one example. In *Inspirations Unbidden: The "Terrible Sonnets" of Gerard Manley Hopkins*, Daniel A. Harris points out that

> the Ignatian exercise is a consciously Trinitarian structure. Its three main episodes—the composition of place, the moral analysis, and the colloquy— correspond to the chief faculties of Augustinian psychology, the memory, the understanding, and the will. The Trinitarian structure makes completion of the exercise—in the soul's willed movement towards God—essential for the recognition of its sacramental nature.

Colloquy is plain in all but three of his sonnets in this period, and is hallmarked by a vocative of affirmation and grace and consolation, as in these concluding lines from "God's Grandeur":

And though the last lights off the black West went
Oh, morning, at the brown brink eastward, springs—
Because the Holy Ghost óver the bent
World broods with warm breast and with ah! bright wings.

Omitting this colloquy in his so-called "terrible sonnets" will be a sign of his feelings of wretchedness and of his loss—like that which afflicted Saint Teresa of Ávila— of any genuine, tangible image of God with which he could freely communicate.

Composed just three months after "God's Grandeur" is "The Windhover," a poem that Hopkins himself regarded as the best thing he ever wrote. About a kind of kestrel, or falcon, and its mastery of flight, "The Windhover," becomes a poem "to

Christ our Lord," his "chevalier," his "dear," whose mastery of weather and earth and humankind are cause for rejoicing. Even poor and ordinary things—field work and crumbling embers—are glorious, having been redeemed by Christ's sacrifice, a bloodshed alluded to in the poem's final line:

No wőnder of it: shéer plód makes plóugh down síllion
Shíne, and blue-bleak embers, ah my dear,
Fall, gáll themsélves, and gásh gőld-vermílion.

Each poem from this period stresses the fulfillment of the Incarnation in the beauty and coherence of nature, as in this final stanza from "Pied Beauty" and its paean to the beauty in diversity:

Áll things counter, original, spare, stránge;
Whatever is fickle, frecklèd (who knows how?)
With swíft, slów; sweet, sóur; adázzle, dím;
He fathers-forth whose beauty is pást chánge:
Práise hím.

Were we talking in terms of marriage, this fresh enthusiasm and bliss and concord with the Holy Being might be likened to his honeymoon. The frailty of his health, his habitual inability to acquit himself well in public settings, and his near failure in his examinations in dogmatic theology finally persuaded his Jesuit superiors that he ought not stay at St. Beuno's for a fourth year of theology, and he was assigned to teach classics and religion to teenagers at Mount St. Mary's College in the bleak countryside near Sheffield. Within a half year he was transferred to Stonyhurst to coach undergraduates in Latin but after four months was shifted again to the Special Preacher's job at the Jesuit church in London's West End. And then for three years he assisted parish priests in foul slums and foundry towns—first in Oxford, then Bedford Leigh, Liverpool, and Glasgow.

We may infer from these frenetic changes that Hopkins was found wanting in his jobs and his superiors were forlornly hunting for the right niche for him. And yet there are few signs of chagrin or disappointment in his poetry. Exhausted as he was by the helping and healing tasks of parish work, Hopkins seems to have found happiness and infusions of grace in his own religious life, and found a unitive way to marry his poetry with pastoral ministry. "Duns Scotus's Oxford," "The Handsome Heart," and "At the Wedding March" were prompted by the satisfactions of his priestly offices, and in "Felix Randal" we see how he felt the affections of the sick while being affected by them, and "tendered" to the dying farrier the Host of viaticum that is "our swéet repríeve and ránsom."

This séeing the síck endéars them tó us, us tóo it endéars.
My tongue had taught thee comfort, touch had quenched thy tears,

Thy tears that touched my heart, child, Félix, poor Felix
Randal;

Walking back from celebrating a Mass at Rosehill, a Catholic country house near Lancashire, Hopkins contemplated Earthly Paradise and found the inspiration for "Spring and Fall: to a Young Child," a haunting fantasy on the "fresh thoughts" of a girl in harmony with nature and of the child's first faint intimations of mortality due to the Fall of humankind—the universal decay from which Christ has rescued us.

Márgarét, áre you gríeving
Over Goldengrove unleaving?
Leáves, líke the thíngs of mán, you
With your fresh thoughts care for, can you?
Áh! ás the héart grows ólder
It will come to such sights colder
By and by, nor spare a sigh
Though worlds of wanwood leafmeal lie;
And yet you will *weep and know why.*
Now no matter, child, the name:
Sórrow's spríngs áre the sáme.
Nor mouth had, no nor mind, expressed
What héart héard of, ghóst guéssed:
It is the blíght mán was bórn for,
It is Margaret you mourn for.

Even in hardship and loss, the God of consolations was present, but we see in "Spring and Fall" the first stains of regret and aridity in the priest—it is Hopkins himself that the poet mourns for.

3. ESTRANGEMENT

In 1881 Hopkins returned to Manresa House in Roehampton in order to reanimate the fervor of his novitiate experience in his tertianship—or, as Saint Ignatius put it, the school of the heart—which included a silent, thirty-day retreat with the *Spiritual Exercises* and nine months that were free for reflection and prayer. At its conclusion, in August 1882, at age thirty-eight, Gerard Manley Hopkins took his final vows as spiritual coadjutor in the Society of Jesus and was posted to a position teaching high school Latin and Greek at Stonyhurst College in Lancashire and then to Ireland for five dreary years as professor of Greek and Latin literature at University College, Dublin.

Entrance into this period of desolation and religious pain is entrance into the period of his highest poetic achievement in the so-called "terrible sonnets," in which Hopkins's sense of Christ's disappearance from his life occasioned radical changes in the structure of his imagery, his use of Ignatian meditation as a formal model, and his relations with his imagined audience.

Saint Ignatius defined just this spiritual desolation in his "Rules for the Discernment of Spirits" in his *Spiritual Exercises*:

> darkness of soul, disturbance in it, movement to things low and earthly, the unquiet of different agitations and

> temptations, moving to want of confidence, without hope, without love, when one finds oneself all lazy, tepid, sad, and as if separated from his Creator and Lord.

Writing a letter to a friend about Duns Scotus, whom he called "the greatest of the divines and doctors of the Church," Hopkins betrays some of his own disillusionment, humiliation, and pain.

> And so I used to feel of Duns Scotus when I used to read him with delight: he saw too far, he knew too much; his subtlety overshot his interests; a kind of feud arose between genius and talent, and the ruck of talent in the Schools finding itself, as his age passed by, less and less able to understand him, voted that there was nothing important to understand . . .

The poetry of his forties betrayed his dissatisfaction and melancholy when he was forced to try to reconcile his bleak emotional judgments with all he had been taught and had himself preached. Hopkins's Christian hope was not in this life, of course, but beyond the grave, in a hidden world veiled in the light of the Holy Being. Sustained by the comfort of Christ's resurrection, Hopkins escaped sheer pessimism, but yielded to a despairing supplication in his poem "(*Justus quidem tu es, Domine*)," a complaint that paraphrased Jeremiah 12:1: "Lord, if I argued my case with you, you would prove to be right. Yet I must question you about matters of justice. Why are wicked men so prosperous? Why do dishonest men succeed?" Hopkins sees only the God of Isaiah, a God who seems hidden, and he is assailed by the false belief that no work of his will ever endure, that in becoming, like Saint Paul, a slave to Jesus Christ, he may have simply become "Time's eunuch." Nature continues in its seasons, birds build content in the knowledge of God; but Hopkins labors in a vain attempt to reach God, realizing only a vast impotence. Echoing Matthew Arnold, the final line is a prayer both for literary immortality and spiritual rebirth. "Mine, O thou lord of life, send my roots rain."

Thou art indeed just, Lord, if I contend
With thee; but, sir, so what I plead is just.
Whý do sínners' ways prosper? and why must
Dísappóintment all I endeavour end?
Wert thou my enemy, O thou my friend,
How wouldst thou worse, I wonder, than thou dost
Defeat, thwart me? Oh, the sots and thralls of lust
Do in spare hours more thrive than I that spend,
Sir, life upon thy cause. See, banks and brakes
Now, leavèd how thick! lacèd they are again
With fretty chervil, look, and the fresh wind shakes
Them; birds build—but not I build; no, but strain,
Time's eunuch, and not breed one work that wakes.
Mine, O thou lord of life, send my roots rain.

And Saint John of the Cross may not have expressed the dark night of the soul better than in this complaint:

No worst, there is none. Pitched past pitch of grief
More pangs will, schooled at forepangs, wilder wring.
Comforter, where, where is your comforting?
Mary, mother of us, where is your relief?

Other "melancholy sonnets"—his own term for them—similarly illustrate his affliction in the desert of Christian growth. We see him write in "(Carrion Comfort)":

Not, I'll not, carrion comfort, Despair, not feast on thee;
Not untwist—slack they may be — these last strands of man
In me ór, most weary, cry I can no more. *I can;*
Can something, hope, wish day come, not choose not to be.

His last line highlights the shock and shame of his position whence "Of now done darkness I wretch lay wrestling with (my God!) my God."

These are stirring and highly successful poems that wonderfully demonstrate the fruits of the desert, for Hopkins was being purified in his suffering and was being taught to desire God for God's sake alone. We see him being transformed as he truly encounters himself in the pathos of his humanity:

He! Hand to mouth he lives, and voids with shame;
And, blazoned in however bold the name,
Man Jack the man is, just; his mate a hussy.

That was "(The shepherd's brow)," a poem composed just two months before his premature death. Earlier, after a January retreat at Saint Stanislaus's College in Tullabeg, he'd written in his journal:

> But how is it with me? I was a Christian from birth to baptism, later I was converted to the Catholic faith, and am enlisted 20 years in the Society of Jesus. I am now 44. I do not waver in my allegiance, I never have since my conversion to the Church. The question is how I advance the side I serve on. This may be inwardly or outwardly. Outwardly I often think I am employed to do what is of little or no use. . . .
>
> Jan. 2—This morning I made the meditation on the Three Sins, with nothing to enter but loathing of my life and a barren submission to God's will. The body cannot rest when it is in pain nor the mind be at peace as long as something bitter distills in it and it aches. . . .
>
> Afternoon: on the same—more loathing and only this thought, that I can do my spiritual and other duties better with God's help.

Five months later, in May 1889, Gerard Manley Hopkins was diagnosed with a kind of typhoid and given an infirmary bed in his Dublin college. On June 8, he foresaw that he was dying and asked for Viaticum. A few hours later some members of his Jesuit community heard him say, "I am so happy, I am so happy," after which he died peacefully, at half past one in the afternoon.

Leo Tolstoy's "Master and Man"

We were far into the old have-you-ever-read? questions. It was August 1991, and Jim Shepard and I were sitting on the shaded second-floor porch of a house at the Bread Loaf Writers' Conference in Vermont, talking about great short stories, the kind that hold you spellbound, make your hair stand on end, that you finish with the feeling of being wrung out, transported, and far better off than you were when you began reading. We lobbed titles at Tim O'Brien, who lobbed a few of his own back. We mentioned "In Dreams Begin Responsibilities" by Delmore Schwartz, "A Distant Episode" by Paul Bowles, Jack London's "To Build a Fire," Shirley Jackson's "The Lottery." Jim and I were two fiction writers on staff at the conference, and university professors in English departments otherwise, so we had read a fair share of the short story masterpieces that find their way into anthologies, but there were so many others that were too little known. We'd both had the experience of having a friend say, "You've got to read this," *as he or she handed us a story we'd never heard of, and on finishing it we'd often wondered how we'd felt complete without it. And countless times we and other writers we knew had been asked in question-and-answer sessions after fiction readings, What are* your *favorite stories? What do* you *recommend?*

Wouldn't it be great, we thought, if there were an anthology based upon the stories that other writers feel passionate about? And that's where our anthology You've Got to Read This *began. We compiled a long list of our favorite writers and wrote to ask if they'd introduce a story that left them breathless, held them in awe, or otherwise enthralled them when they first read it. We approached some very famous and busy people so it was no surprise that a good many begged off, but a far greater number were pleased to have been asked and supplied us with a roster of one or three or six or nine stories they'd be happy to introduce.*

We were then faced with hard choices, some of them frankly financial but others having to do with balance and variety and our own highly subjective judgment of which were the greater masterpieces. Often the decisions were painful. We could have filled another anthology with the stories we had to reject or could not afford, but we finally came up with just what we wanted: the familiar and the unfamiliar, the hundred-years-old and the just-yesterday, stories that are symphonies of emotion and stories that are the simplest of melodies, beautifully played. Seeing the masterpieces that were missing, we two editors then had the privilege of making our own selections of masterpieces that we felt a first-rate anthology could not do without. Jim's choice was Vladimir Nabokov's "Spring in Fialta" and mine was Leo Tolstoy's "Master and Man."

LEO TOLSTOY'S "MASTER AND MAN"

With *War and Peace*, *Anna Karenina*, and "The Death of Ivan Ilych," "Master and Man" is generally considered one of Leo Tolstoy's greatest masterpieces, though one would never guess that from his diary entries about it. "I have now written the rough draft of a not very interesting story," he initially noted, "but it helped me to while away the time." Weeks later while further revising it he wrote, "Don't know whether it is good. Very insignificant." Still later he was concerned that the content was "feeble," and that "it is no good. No character—neither the one nor the other." Even after a favorite editor accepted "Master and Man," Tolstoy was so pained about his failure with it that he wrote a friend, "I have sinned with the story I sent off to *The Northern Messenger*. I write 'I have sinned' because I am ashamed to have wasted my time on such stuff."

Written in the fall of 1894 and fully revised thirteen times before he finally surrendered it to publication in 1895, the story is set some twenty years earlier in order to give it the flavor of a legend or folk tale. "*Khozyain i rabotnik*," its Russian title, could be translated literally as "Householder and Laborer" but for the story's Christian underpinnings, which insist on the terms of the Gospels, where Jesus is often referred to as Master and humanity in general is the subject of his parables. And a parable "Master and Man" surely is, a highly metaphoric but accessible tale of common life whose purpose is the spiritual conversion of its audience.

We miss, in our English translations, the high-flown historical tone of the first pages gradually giving way to a plainer, ingenuous style and the urgency of the present tense. We miss, too, the significance of the names. The second guild merchant Vassili Brekhunoff's last name is from the Russian term for a braggart or liar, his village is Kresti, the Crosses, and Nikita, of course, must have been christened in honor of Saint Nicholas, the fourth-century Turkish bishop and wonderworker whose cult provided the basis for our Santa Claus. Like Charles Dickens's "A Christmas Carol," with which Tolstoy was familiar, "Master and Man" features a haughty employer who only feels contempt for his lowly hired hand but finally has his world view upset as he learns how to live and to love.

When Leo Tolstoy was first famous at twenty-nine, Ivan Turgenev characterized him as a "poet, Calvinist, fanatic, aristocrat." At age sixty-six, when he wrote "Master and Man," Count Tolstoy was changed only in having given up Calvinism for a fanatical Christian religion wholly his own and having forfeited a great deal of his wealth and prestige in order to live, to his mind, the holy life of a *muzhik*, or peasant.

At fifty-five he'd written, in *What I Believe*, that he'd been from the age of fifteen to fifty a Nihilist, or one who has no religious beliefs.

> Five years ago I began to believe in the teaching of Jesus Christ, and my life was suddenly changed. I ceased to care for all that I had formerly desired, and began to long for

> what I had once cared nothing for. What had before seemed good, seemed bad, and what had seemed bad, now seemed good. That happened to me which might happen to a man, who, having left his home on business, should suddenly realize that the business was unnecessary and should go home again.

Adopting a metaphor that he would take up again in his great short story, Tolstoy wrote still later in *What I Believe* of the conflicting urges in his own psychology at the time of his religious conversion:

> I am lost in a snowstorm. One of my companions assures me that he sees lights in the distance and that there is a village. But it is only a delusion, which we believe because we wish to do so. We have searched for those lights and cannot find them. Another comrade goes looking about in the snow, and at last he reaches the road, and cries to us, "Do not go on, the lights you see are in your own fancy; you will but wander about and perish. Here is the road, I am standing on it, and it will lead us to safety." It is very little. While we believed in the lights that shone only in our bewildered eyes we foresaw ourselves in the village, in a warm hut, safe and at rest. Now we have nothing but the hard road. But if we follow the false lights we must surely perish: if we follow the road, we shall surely be saved.

"Master and Man" can be read as a fictional elaboration of that metaphor, positing, in Brekhunoff, Tolstoy's self-portrait of pride, independence, waywardness, and death and, in Nikita, his hoped-for future self of simplicity, participation, certitude, and the firm road to life everlasting. Brekhunoff fancies himself formidable and self-sufficient, but in crisis he's hapless, selfish, and lost, a church elder whose religious feelings have been a sham, and a scheming businessman whose intrigues are useless in the wilds. Nikita has no illusions about himself. Wholly lacking in possessions, importance, or aspirations, scorned as an "old fool," a drunkard, and cuckold, Nikita is free to be affectionate, genuine, humble, in harmony with nature, faithful to God, and unafraid of death. Tolstoy's own fierce struggle for human integrity and religious consolation is given form in these hugely different men who ultimately find and heed the same life force.

The plot is wonderfully simple. Merchant and hired man head off for a village but so often get lost in a harrowing snowstorm that they have to wait out the night in their sledge. Brekhunoff selfishly tries to flee on the horse, but fate brings him back to the freezing Nikita. Brekhunoff's first impulse is to protect Nikita from the cold as he would any of his properties, but when he offers his heated body to the old peasant and feels Nikita reviving beneath him, Brekhunoff is gradually changed. "Then he began to think about his money, his store, his house, his sales and purchases, and Mironoff's millions. He could not understand how that man whom men called Vassili Brekhunoff could bear to interest himself in such things as he did." Earlier he'd felt "to live" (*zhit'*) was "to acquire" (*nazhit'*), but as

Brekhunoff selflessly sacrifices himself for Nikita, he is fulfilled by Christ's gospel message that "'Greater love has no man than this, that a man lay down his life for his friends.'"

Tolstoy annihilated a great deal of fiction for me with "Master and Man." Everything I'd been reading up till then seemed petty and unimportant. Like Brekhunoff I could not understand how I could bear to interest myself in such things as I did. It was in the seventies, in winter; I was a first-year graduate student at the University of Iowa's Writers Workshop, and fat flakes of snow were softly falling as I hiked the two miles to Vance Bourjaily's afternoon class on Tolstoy's masterpieces. And as I hunched forward in a Russian cold with Tolstoy's story in my head, I felt challenged to be the kind of writer he was but also haunted by the fear that my standard was now too high.

And so it was for Tolstoy, too. Except for a handful of fables and the flawed novel, *Resurrection*, "Master and Man" was the last fictional work Leo Tolstoy would publish. Two years after the story appeared, he argued in *What Is Art?* that the highest form of art was religious and, under that aesthetic, condemned his own great works of fiction up to that point as failures. He feuded with his wife, Sofya, and his family of thirteen children over their life of ease on his grand estate at Yasnaya Polyana and in accordance with the faith he professed tried to give away all he owned and to be more and more like a peasant. At last, in late October 1910, Tolstoy took flight from his estate hoping to find refuge and religious consolation in an eastern monastery, and he was on his way there when he died of pneumonia in the railroad station in Astapovo, Riazan, at the age of eighty-two.

Tolstoy's dying must have seemed to him a good deal like Nikita's—not at home, but with *ikons* and candles, his wife left behind but forgiven, his focus wholly on "that other life which had been growing more and more familiar and alluring." Whether Tolstoy was disillusioned or found what he expected, we shall all soon know.

Babette's Feast

I have learned a lot from film. In fact, if asked who my foremost influences were as a writer I would be niggardly if I did not include great directors like Ingmar Bergman or François Truffaut. I have seen many more movies than I have read novels, by a margin of probably five to one, so it would be strange if my writing did not reflect a cinematic style.

I still remember the first time I saw Citizen Kane *on television as a boy. It was just a summer's late night slot filler in Omaha, and there was no one to introduce it as a classic, and inane commercials knifed into it in stupid and insulting ways, but flat on my belly, my chin in my hands, I stayed with it, fully engrossed, to the final shot on Kane's sled. "Oh, wow!" I said to Rob beside me. "Rosebud was the* sled's *name!" Rob got it, too. Wide-eyed and breathless, he and I went upstairs to bed still talking about the structure and scenes, not in that "Wasn't it cool when . . . ?" way of the science fiction and monster movies we favored, but with a consideration and admiration that we didn't yet have the words for. I felt smarter for having watched it.*

The same thing happened, differently, the first time I saw King Kong *and* Beau Geste *and* The Maltese Falcon. *But I was still too young to have the vocabulary to say why I thought a film was perfect. And what I could not express seemed to stew in me like the pining for love.*

At Creighton Preparatory School, a few of the younger Jesuit instructors started a Sunday night club called the Foreign Film Forum. We'd sit at milk-stained lunch tables in the cafeteria to watch films like The Seventh Seal, Closely Watched Trains, *and* The Bicycle Thief, *and afterwards we'd be guided through a discussion of the social and religious themes underlying the surface of desire and desperation and white-lettered subtitles. We were teenagers so our conversations were fairly basic, but through them I was given a language and way of seeing that changed how I viewed things on the screen. It was one of the high points of high school for me.*

I have since written six screenplays, visited a number of film sets and editing rooms, been ferried from place to place in chauffeured limousines, and when I watch the Academy Award telecasts I am often rooting for friends. I am, on occasion, in the business. But a great film can still leave me wide-eyed and breathless. Such a film is Babette's Feast, *which I wrote about for my friend Jim Shepard's anthology* Writers on Film: Twenty-six Contemporary Authors Celebrate Twenty-six Memorable Movies.

BABETTE'S FEAST

After a glorious but expensive vacation in Venice in 1949, the Danish storyteller Karen Blixen considered writing fiction specifically for the high-paying American magazine market. An

English visitor to the Baroness's estate of Rungstedlund, northeast of Copenhagen, challenged her to do so by wagering that she could not sell a story to the *Saturday Evening Post,* and she took the bet, though she was not sure what American magazines wanted.

"Write about food," the Englishman said, for she'd been trained in the culinary arts in Paris, she was justly famous for her lavish, gourmet dinner parties, and even news magazines like *Life* carried recipes then. But there may have been a hint of nasty irony in his suggestion as well, for Karen Blixen was then habitually ill—she'd contracted syphilis from her ex-husband many years earlier—and she ate so little that she was just skin and bones, weighing less than ninety pounds.

She wrote "Babette's Feast" in English, the language in which she first told tales to her lover, the late Denys Finch-Hatton, an Oxford-educated trader and wilderness guide in East Africa who considered Karen his Scheherazade. She may have modeled the character of Madame Babette Hersant at least partially on Clara Svendsen, a well-educated Catholic schoolteacher from the north of Denmark who so loved Karen Blixen's books that she gave up her home and job to serve as the Baroness's maid, secretary, nurse, and literary executor. Karen seems to have based the self-willed, sophisticated, and introspective General Lorens Loewenhielm on the life and thought of the Danish philosopher Søren Kierkegaard and on her restless, much-revered father, Captain Wilhelm Dinesen, who'd served in the Franco-Prussian war and in 1871 witnessed the Marquis de Gallifet's vicious persecution and slaughter of the insurrectionist Communards of Paris. Elements of her mother's puritanical side of the family probably influenced her depiction of two pious, unmarried sisters whose falling in love was as welcomed as child sacrifice. Even the story's location on a Norwegian fjord seems to have been chosen as a look-alike for the Jutland heaths she visited as a child.

In Karen Blixen's suave comedy, Madame Babette Hersant is a famous chef at the Café Anglais who flees Paris after the execution of her husband and son in the 1871 civil war and winds up in a desolate settlement in Norway. Working as a humble cook and housekeeper for two sweet and devout spinsters who have forsaken offers of marriage, wealth, pleasure, and fame to minister to a radically puritanical Lutheran sect established by their father, she's expected to prepare only frugal meals of salted codfish and ale-bread soup. But when, after fourteen years of service, Babette wins ten thousand francs in a lottery, she chooses to spend it all in a magnificent feast that will celebrate the hundredth anniversary of the sisters' late father's birthday.

Seeing the exotic foods and wines grandly arriving from Paris in wheelbarrows, one sister goes out to their congregation, urging them to take no notice of this high cuisine for fear of offending God. One old man promises her, "'We will cleanse our tongues of all taste and purify them of all delight or disgust of the senses, keeping and preserving them for the higher things of praise and thanksgiving.'"

But an epicurean Army general who once was in love with

one of the sisters has also been invited to the feast, and is bewildered to see his fellow diners consuming the finest Amontillado and turtle soup and Blinis Demidoff "without any sign of either surprise or approval, as if they had been doing so every day for thirty years."

Elated by Babette's artistry, the general offers a toast that he first heard from the Dean whose hundredth anniversary they are celebrating, and which he finally understands. "Mercy and truth, my friends, have met together," General Loewenhielm says. "Righteousness and bliss shall kiss one another."

Resentments and discord had begun to divide the old and failing congregation, but as they gradually give up their self-abnegation during Babette's feast, the dinner guests forgive each other and wind up outside, holding hands like children under the starlight as they sing a hymn of paradise.

"Babette's Feast" merges incongruities, reconciles the irreconcilable. With Søren Kierkegaard, Karen Blixen argues against the either/or proposition that there is only one correct way to live one's life, that we are faced with a series of critical choices and if we choose wrongly we are lost. In her story the hedonistic general finds in the miracle of Babette's feast both ecstatic pleasure and a joyful, magnanimous God whom he otherwise could not have imagined. The congregation of fractious Puritans who chose a difficult, self-denying spirituality for themselves find in the feast the religious ecstasy they have sought and the sensual pleasure they have shunned. And Babette is satisfied because, as she says, she is "a great artist" and this is what she does, whether or not there are those who can fully savor it.

Karen Blixen lost the wager. Employing the male pseudonym of Isak Dinesen—"he who laughs" plus her maiden name—she submitted "Babette's Feast" to the *Saturday Evening Post*, but the editors rejected it, as did the editors of *Good Housekeeping*, who felt it concentrated too much on the upper classes who were, presumably, not their readership. She finally did manage to sell the story to the *Ladies' Home Journal,* where it appeared in May 1950.

She was sixty-five years old then. And Gabriel Axel was nearly seventy when he scripted and directed its winsome screen adaptation, *Babettes Gæstebud*, the Academy Award winner for the best foreign film of 1987. It's perhaps not surprising, then, that *Babette's Feast* focuses its gentle humor on the frailties, anxieties, and self-recriminations of the aging, while quietly congratulating its characters for their generosity, loyalty, religious conviction, humility, sanity, and self-discipline—qualities that are not often saluted in film.

My friend Jim Shepard was the first to alert me to the ways in which *Babette's Feast* slyly plays with the conventions of the American movies that were called "women's pictures": sentimental melodramas like *Imitation of Life* and *Stella Dallas* about intense emotions being bottled up, about lives not fully lived, about heroines who abandon or deny their own wishes, dreams, ambitions, or dangerous stirrings of the heart in subordination to another person or in soulful obedience to an interior code of morality and conscience.

In the film *Babette's Feast*, as in Blixen's tale, the main protagonists are Martine and Filippa, sisters named in reverence for the German Protestant reformers Martin Luther and Philipp Melanchthon. The sisters' adored father was the founder of a puritanical Lutheran sect in a gray, dull, huddled village on the Jutland heaths, but now the Dean, as he was called, is long dead and his elderly daughters devote all their hours and inherited income on good works for a dwindling number of crotchety disciples. But there was a time many years ago when the hands of the girls were sought by bachelors who went to church just to see them, for the strikingly beautiful girls did not go to parties or balls. The Dean (Pouel Kern) rejected their many suitors with the excuse that his daughters were his only handmaids, but in fact his theology was such that earthly love and marriage were thought to be of little worth, an illusion.

And yet there *were* romantic moments for them. A vain lieutenant in the hussars (Gudmar Wivesson), whose debts caused him to be banished to his aunt's manor for three months, chanced to see Martine (Vibeke Hastrup) while he was horseback riding and he instantly fell in love with the idea of the higher, purer life she so attractively seemed to offer. She was largely imaginary, of course, just a projection of all he was not; and he may have been a soldierly fantasy for Martine, who was curious about, if not excited by, the intensity of his interest. But in the end she saw Lorens Loewenhielm walk away with a cold if chivalrous goodbye. "I have learned here that life is hard and cruel," he said, "and that in this world there are things that are impossible." Lorens would go off and marry a lady-in-waiting to Queen Sophia, wear a monocle and recite high-sounding pieties, and rise in rank and importance in the Swedish royal court. Whereas Martine would stay in the village, doing the things she'd always done, sharing a bedroom with her sister; and if she did not pine for the handsome lieutenant, she did still remember him with nostalgia and silent pleasure.

Filippa (Hanne Stensgard) was wooed by Monsieur Achille Papin (Jean-Philippe Lafont), an "*Artiste Lyrique*" who left the Royal Opera in Stockholm to vacation in the silence and vacancy of the Jutland coast, but was so stunned at hearing Filippa's gorgeous singing in church that he introduced himself to the Dean and offered his services as a voice coach, saying she was a diva who'd have Paris at her feet. Although concerned that Achille Papin was a Roman Catholic, a papist, Filippa's father consented, but worriedly listened with Martine as the singers joined in an insouciant duet about passion and desire. Filippa did not betray her father. Seemingly flustered by the tenor's flattery and her own unfamiliar sexual feelings, and all too aware that the success Achille wanted for her would only constitute a loss to the village and the common good, she sacrificed her still incipient artistic aspirations and satisfied the Dean by announcing she wished to discontinue her singing lessons. The grocer with whom the Frenchman was staying gladly delivered the message, and Papin exited their world with the maudlin sigh, "Goodbye, my life, my heart, my hopes."

The softness of touch in this first act is wonderful. It all could have gone so wrong. The father could have been one of those hellhound men of religion that the movies have been giving us in Crayola colors ever since *Elmer Gantry* and *Night of the Hunter.* Martine could have been jilted and pregnant, and Filippa could have run off with Achille in some corny variant on *A Star Is Born* or *Beaches.* Even without the sensationalism that some screenwriters are prey to, there could have been those errors of judgment, stress, and psychological analysis that actors too often fall into: their own anger, pain, and manias seething anachronistically through nineteenth century characters who would be, and are, far more serene with their lot.

We have the holiness and gracefulness of Martine and Filippa in old age as evidence that theirs is not a hackneyed story of wasted talent, sexual repression, or that old domineering dad we stew so much about. Rather it is about balance, harmony, and prayerful consciousness, with freedom and boundaries, desire and discipline, joy and sorrow equally distributed for them as they are for everyone. When I first saw *Babette's Feast* I was cautiously waiting for one of those shammed and cynical moments to spoil it, and part of the lift I felt when I left this sweetest of films was in the realization that Gabriel Axel and his actors were so reasonable, restrained, and respectful of the usualness of life.

The second act of *Babette's Feast* begins with a sound bridge and a darkening, and the film leaps ahead to a rainstorm on a September night in 1871. We see a hooded woman (Stephane Audran) struggle and tilt forward through the muck of a village street. Either a waif or a figure of death. She knocks at the door of the now much older sisters (Birgitte Federspiel and Bodil Kjer), is invited in, and seems to faint on their couch. Reading a letter of introduction from Monsieur Achille Papin, they find out that Madame Babette Hersant, like Empress Eugénie, has been forced to flee Paris due to civil war. "She, herself, narrowly escaped the blood-stained hands of General Gallifet," Achille writes. Imagining Filippa's world as child-filled, happy, and full of honors—she twinges with the sting of that irony as she hears it—Achille writes of his own loneliness and lost fame and insists it was Filippa who chose the better path in life. She secretly wonders. Consoling himself as well as her, Achille writes, "In Paradise I shall hear your voice again. There you will forever be the great artist God intended you to be. Oh, how you will enchant the angels!" And then in comic understatement, his letter concludes with the laconic postscript, "Babette knows how to cook."

Babette agrees to work for no wages, saying, "If you won't let me serve you, I will simply die." She seems to mean she needs their food and shelter, but the film will finally require us to give emphasis to the gravity of that word "serve." We see it the next morning as Martine schools their servant in soaking their stale bread in ale and softening a filet of cod that looks like the sole of a shoe. We'll learn later that Babette is a culinary genius, yet she now neither winces nor worries at their cuisine, she just calmly takes it all in. She is kin to those stoic missionaries who eat and drink whatever is set before them.

Babette gradually learns the Danish language. She learns to haggle with the fishmonger, to gently criticize the grocer for selling her rancid bacon. She pensively strolls along a jade green hillside at sundown—one golden, luminous frame was used for the movie poster—and we notice that the palette has changed, the wintry tones of the film's first act having given way to rich pastel shades of peach and saffron. She's the image of dignity and self-knowledge. She imitates the sisters whose Christian crosses ride on their chests, but she wears the Catholic form of the sacramental, with Christ crucified on it, and we have to decide for ourselves if it's an ecumenical act of solidarity or one of silent opposition. She may be miserable in this Jutland village, but she's mute about it. Even her lovely face is difficult to read: is she just naturally solemn or is she indeed forlorn? And we wonder if anyone in the village has thought to ask.

In voice-over an old narrator who is meant to sound like Isak Dinesen informs us that fourteen years have passed since Babette joined the minister's daughters, so it's 1885—the year, interestingly, of Karen Dinesen's birth. The congregation is not only older but comically cantankerous, and without the late Dean's prophetic vision and stern governance they have only a crabbed and remembered form of religion, not its substance, and they're now wrecking their weekly conferences with pettiness, strife, and recriminations.

To heal their differences, Martine announces the dinner to honor the Dean's hundreth birthday. And in the way of tales, in just the same week, Babette learns she's won ten thousand francs in the French lottery. The sisters try to be happy about Babette's good fortune, but they presume she'll now leave them, just as have the men with whom they've been affectionate. But Babette has yet to say what she'll do. She goes to the seashore to give it some thought, and, in a nice visual metaphor for prayer, the camera tracks a white gull skimming just above the North Sea. Quickly deciding, she strides purposefully back to the house and, squeezing the crucifix at her neck, she asks the sisters one favor: "I would like to prepare the celebration dinner for the minister's birthday by myself."

She orders the ingredients from France and we watch the food and drink arriving in all their luxurious plenitude: a slat cage holding nervous quail; caviar, perhaps, in an oblong block of ice; a slowly blinking sea turtle; a box of fragile glassware; a case of *grand cru* Clos de Vougeot that has aged forty years.

Seeing the exorbitance, Martine is troubled enough that she has a hellish nightmare that unites in a comic, excessive way the fatted calf of the Bible, a pen-and-ink drawing of the grim reaper, and a vision of blood-red wine spilling from a tankard as a drunk falls facedown on a dinner table. Wakening, Martine connects Babette's proposed feast with sensuality, evil powers, and the makings of a witch's Sabbath, and she privately instructs the congregation to negate their senses and give the food and drink no attention, a *via negativa* that already seems to have been central to their religious practice.

Eleven from the village are guests at the feast. The twelfth guest is General Lorens Loewenhielm (Jarl Kulle), now an eminence in the Swedish royal court whom we find in the manor of the aged aunt he is visiting. Adjusting a monocle in his left eye, he quotes Ecclesiastes as he tells himself in the mirror, "Vanity. All is vanity." And then he turns and sees himself as the lovesick young hussar he once was. "I have found everything you dreamed of and satisfied your ambition but to what purpose?" he asks himself. "Tonight we two shall settle our score. You must prove to me that the choice I made was the right one."

Meanwhile, Babette is cooking, and cinematographer Henning Kristiansen's camera cherishes each confident touch of food preparation, noticing in the once stark kitchen colors that are now as vivid and opulent as in a painting by Caravaggio: red meats, magenta wine, the jet black beads of spooned caviar, steaming copper cauldrons and skillets, Babette's auburn hair; and, in the dining room, a snow-white tablecloth, shining crystal, and the silver cutlery and candlesticks she's purchased for the occasion.

Upon arrival, the faithful of the sect join hands in the parlor to sing yet again a hymn we have heard many times, but that they seem not to have listened to: *Jerusalem, my heart's true home / Your name is ever dear to me / Your kindness is second to none / You keep us clothed and fed / Never would you give a stone / to the child who begs for bread.*

And then they go warily into the dining room, wanting, it would seem, stones. Shocked by the extravagance as they begin their first course, one of the faithful whispers, "Remember . . . we have lost our sense of taste."

A gray-bearded villager agrees, "Like the wedding at Cana. The food is of no importance."

Cana, near Nazareth, was the location of a postwedding feast in the Gospel account of John (2:1–11), in which the mother of Jesus informs her son that the host has run out of wine, and Jesus graciously turns the water in six stone jars into the finest wine the steward has tasted. The old villager is right: food is never mentioned in that Gospel passage. But there's something crucially wrong with the interpretation that the food and the wine are of no importance, only the miracle, the sign. It's an anti-incarnational sentiment that ignores Mary and her son's solicitude for the host's sudden embarrassment—though a good deal of wine must have been consumed there already—and strangely implies that the natural world that God brought into being is in some way an impediment to achieving the joys of heaven. *Babette's Feast* will say otherwise.

General Loewenhielm has no such misgivings about the good things of life, and is gratified to have been served the finest amontillado he's ever tasted, real turtle soup, perfectly fashioned Blinis Demidoff, and an 1860 Veuve Clicquot champagne that the villagers seem to think is a variety of lemonade. Stunned by the magnificent quality of the feast, and hearing stories of the Dean's wisdom and miracles, the general intrudes on the villagers' mild reminiscences to narrate one of his own: that of a memorable dinner with some French officers at the Café Anglais in Paris where the head chef served them a dish of her own creation, *Cailles en Sarcophage.* And he mentions that General Gallifet, his host, told him that the head chef could transform a dinner into a love affair in which no distinction was made between the sensual and spiritual appetites. Seemingly unaware of the irony, Lorens goes on to say that General Gallifet—the man, we recall, who executed Babette's husband and son—swore that the head chef at the Café Anglais was the only woman he'd consider shedding his blood for. She was *the* greatest culinary genius. And then Lorens smiles down at the quail in a pastry shell they are now eating. "*This* is *Cailles en Sarcophage*!"

Yet Lorens is so self-involved, and possibly disdainful of the hinterlands of Denmark, that he never questions who the chef in *this* kitchen is; nor do the villagers now give recognition to the author of the feast, though the general has given them good reason to take pride in their friend Babette. It's as if the food materializes from behind the kitchen door for them, without a source, without cost. Even as the guests begin to yield and delight in the feast, a smug village woman still insists, "Man shall not merely refrain from, but also reject any thought of food and drink. Only then can he eat and drink in the proper spirit." And then she simpers with self-satisfaction and sips some wildly expensive burgundy wine.

Axel devotes nineteen minutes—nearly one-fifth of the film—to Babette's haute cuisine, intercutting between the sheer pleasure of the diners, whose differences are mending under the influence of good food and wine, and the sheer labor of Babette, who seems content to practice her art without congratulation. Enough for her to get grins and swooning looks of ecstasy from the carriage driver who brought the general and his aunt, and who sits in the kitchen with Babette, hungrily sampling things and helping by grinding coffee beans.

Right after the enjoyment of the grapes that are meant to cleanse the palate, the general is so transfigured by the generosity and art of this foretaste of the heavenly banquet that he chimes his wineglass and stands to offer a toast. Quoting a favorite passage of the minister they're celebrating, Lorens recites from the King James version of Psalm 85, "Mercy and truth have met together. Righteousness and bliss shall kiss one another." Echoing Søren Kierkegaard, and sharing with the other guests the clarity and self-forgiveness seemingly induced in him by the graciousness of Babette's feast, Lorens indicates that, ideally, faith and ethics, plenty and discipline, love and responsibility are joined. Earlier he'd asked his aunt, "Could many years of victories result in defeat?" And now he realizes that God is much larger than the grudging bookkeeper he'd imagined. We all have anxieties about what we choose to do in life, he says, but our choice is of less importance once we realize that God's mercy is infinite, and that whatever we have sacrificed—whether it be marriage, children, artistic success, or career—will be given back to us in this world or the next. We need only await mercy in confidence and receive it in gratitude.

We may be hard on him elsewhere, but here the general gets it. The feast has converted him. Just as he educated the other guests on the etiquette of spooning the sauce of Blinis Demidoff or crunching the cranium of a quail to suck out its sweet brain, Lorens educates the villagers in an unimaginable forgiveness, and encourages them to see this exquisite feast, this sinful indulgence they so worried about, as a sign of God's magnificent love and grace.

Retiring to a parlor for postprandial champagne and coffee, the jolly guests exchange blessings as Filippa sits at the piano and sings a lullaby about nighttime and rest that is especially apt for the old: "*The sand in our hourglass will soon run out / The day is conquered by the night / The glories of the world are ending / So brief their day, so swift their flight / God, let Thy brightness ever shine / Admit us Thy mercy divine.*"

At song's end, Lorens and his aunt rise to go home, and the

others join them. Holding, as in a wedding, a flaming white candle between them, Martine hesitates at the door with the general, and in a medium close-up that rhymes with the lovesick lieutenant's goodbye to her many years earlier, Lorens now says, "I have been with you every day of my life. Tell me you know that."

She nods and says yes, and we understand just how much she's taken secret pleasure in memories of him.

Lorens declares that from this night forward he will dine with her, not with his body, which is unimportant, but with his soul. "Because this evening I have learned, my dear, that in this beautiful world of ours all things are possible." Precisely the opposite of what he'd stated as a gloomy young man.

Martine gently nods, and he kisses her hand before solemnly going off, saying not a word to the cook.

Walking out into the cold, starlit night, the tipsy sisters and brothers of the congregation hold hands and sing a children's lullaby as they dance around the village well. And then Martine and Filippa find their way to the kitchen to finally thank Babette for the "very good" dinner. Sitting there alone and silent, her elbows on her thighs, Babette seems haggard but content in a job well done. Receiving the sisters' naive praise, she seems to remember other nights of adulation long ago in France, and confirms that she overheard Lorens as he talked of her enemy, Gallifet, by revealing what she's kept secret thus far, that she was once the head chef at the Café Anglais. She says nothing about the emotions she must have felt as she served the friend of her husband and son's executioner. She just goes into the dining room to clear the table, where she shocks the sisters by saying she won't be returning to Paris, for the people she knew there are dead, and anyway she spent all the lottery money on the feast. "Dinner for twelve at the Café Anglais costs ten thousand francs."

The sisters are aghast that she's given all she owned for them, but she smiles and answers it was *not* just for them.

"Now you'll be poor the rest of your life," Martine says.

"An artist is never poor," Babette says, and she quotes Achille Papin: "Throughout the world sounds one long cry from the heart of the artist: Give me the chance to do my very best."

"But this is not the end, Babette," says Filippa. "I'm certain it is not." She recalls Achille Papin's consoling statement about the singing career she'd given up as she says, "In Paradise you will be the great artist that God meant you to be." Eyes welling with tears, she hugs Babette as she says, "Oh, how you will delight the angels!"

Babette's Feast can be looked at in a purely secular way as a glorious testimony to artistic passion and the intoxicating effect that the fine arts can have on those who have learned to pay attention. But it is also a highly metaphorical representation of liturgy, of the Christian recognition of God's graciousness for which thanksgiving is offered in our eucharistic celebrations. Babette is, in many ways, a Christ figure, a mysterious sojourner in the village who forsakes her heritage and becomes a common servant until she hosts a Last Supper for twelve disciples in which their hungers and longings find satisfaction.

Religious faith enriches *Babette's Feast*, but is not necessary for its esteem, for in plainer terms Karen Blixen's tale and Gabriel Axel's screenplay and film are masterpieces of awareness, of seeing into the middle of things, of saying yes to existence and the exaltations of art.

"Anima Christi"

"Anima Christi" *is not a children's prayer. We memorized a host of prayers when I was in grade school, but that wasn't one of them. My favorite when I was nine or so was the worried and emotional one to Michael the Archangel—whose name I would later take at my Confirmation—and who I prayed would defend me in battle and protect me from the wickedness and snares of the devil.*

I first encountered "Anima Christi" *when I read Ignatius of Loyola's* Spiritual Exercises *some years after college and saw it there on the very first page. And for a while I, like many others, thought it was one of Ignatius's inventions, when in fact it was just one that expressed the goal of the exercises especially well. What fascinated me about the prayer called* "Anima Christi" *was that the more I recited it to myself, the less simple it became. Questions kept occurring to me; wider vistas opened up. And because I do not know what I think until I see what I say, I wrote this meditation.*

"ANIMA CHRISTI"

Anima Christi, sanctifica me.
"Soul of Christ, sanctify me."

I have stopped in this great prayer many times upon saying that or upon hearing that I have said it. Four words, and yet all but one, that familiar, half-known *me*, seem to demand firmer definitions.

Christ is, of course, a synecdoche that implies the historical Jesus of Nazareth, held by his followers to be the fulfillment of the Old Testament prophecies concerning the Messiah. *Christos* is, in fact, a rendering in Greek of the Hebrew *mashiach*, meaning the anointed one, the chosen.

Christians participate and share in the priestly, prophetic, and kingly roles of Christ through their own choosing and anointing in the initiatory sacraments of Baptism, Eucharist, and Confirmation, so it is frankly possible to read the prayer's first and following references to Christ in a fuller and more inclusive way as Church. Saint Paul instructed the Colossians to picture Christ as the head of a Church that is his body, and that unity is fundamental in all Christian religious practices. We are praying *Anima Ecclesiae, sanctifica me* as soon as we become catechumens, and the Church saves, hears, defends, and comforts Christians throughout the hardships of their lives. And yet the inspired medieval poet who created this prayer here seems to be writing about Christ the Redeemer, the perfected, post-resurrectional Jesus, King of Kings, Lord of Lords, Son of God and Son of Man, fully divine and everlasting, our quickening, healing, forgiving, and animating principle.

Anima can be properly translated as either soul or spirit or life, but the Latin literally means that which blows or that which is breathed. Wind, in other words. Air. Carl Jung complicated the term even further in his psychology of human personality both by contrasting it with persona and by calling it the inner personality that is fastened to and the force behind our unconscious minds. We are here to others in our personas; we are here to ourselves in our animas.

We could put *Anima Christi* this way then: Wind of Christ, Air that we breathe of Christ, Thereness of Christ, Is-ness of Christ, Truth of Christ, Self-consciousness of Christ, What we do not know of Christ, Christ's understanding of himself: sanctify me.

Ecclesiastical leaders invented the Latin verb *sanctificare*—meaning to make holy, to consecrate, to set apart, to free from sin or purify. There is an interesting linking then between Christ, the anointed one, and we who are anointed and freed from sin and hallowed in the Christian rites of initiation. Christ, the prayer says, make me Christ just as you did at my christening. We are seeking holiness both as a position and as a permanent action. We are asking for specialness through Christ's intercession; to be tapped, signed up, pointed out, invited, included, hired on, excepted, chosen just as he was. Each of those things are first acts from which others follow, the first tottering steps we take as we prepare to walk with God, so it is wonderfully right and fitting that the writer thought to hint at them in his first line.

Corpus Christi, salve me.
"Body of Christ, save me."

We have three yoked concepts in *Corpus Christi*: Christ as human being, Christ as Host or blessed and consecrated bread, and Christ as mystically embodied in the Church. We were saved in a mysterious way by Christ's crucifixion and physical death on the cross; we are helped and preserved and sustained through the real presence of Christ in the Eucharist; a Church inspired by the Holy Spirit keeps us from harm or loss through wise precepts and ordinances; and we share in Christ himself when we join together as Church in his name.

The Solemnity of Corpus Christi Sunday develops the powerfully emblematic idea of Christ being not only body and blood, but fully comparable to and in keeping with the bread and wine offered by the king and high priest, Melchizedek, and the sweet manna that fed the afflicted Israelites in their flight from Egypt. And in his first letter to the Corinthians, Saint Paul writes: "The bread that we break, is it not a sharing in the body of Christ? Because there is one bread, we who are many are one body, for we all partake of the one bread." (1 Cor 10:16–17.)

Every reading on Corpus Christi Sunday highlights again and again the tangible images of blessing, offering, partaking, and feeding. We can imagine a good rough draft of the "*Anima Christi*" that hit those images, too, but "body of Christ, feed me" or ". . . let me partake of thee" would have been both trite and unintelligent, for then the prayer would have been simply puttering with Christ's words of Consecration: "*Accipite, et manducate ex hoc omnes: Hoc est enim Corpus meum.*" Take you, and eat of this: for this is my body.

Whoever wrote the "*Anima Christi*" flatters us by presuming our familiarity with the Latin Mass in order to impress upon us the Christology in the sixth chapter of the Gospel according to John, a Christology that is fundamental to Catholic thinking about the place of the Eucharist in its celebrations: Jesus said to the crowds, "I am the bread of life. Your ancestors ate the manna in the wilderness, and they died. This is the bread that comes down from heaven, so that one may eat of it and not die . . . Whoever eats of this bread will live forever; and the bread that I will give for the life of the world is my flesh." (Jn 6:48–51.)

We are not just afflicted with hankerings and hunger, we are afflicted with an annihilation that may come at any hour. And in that case *salve me* carries with it a hint of desperation and the haunting emphasis of a scream heard in darkness.

Sanguis Christi, inebria me.
"Blood of Christ, inebriate me."

• • •

Intoxicate me. Excite me. Exhilarate me. Saturate me. Convert me. Rule and overwhelm me. Transubstantiate me.

We cannot read *inebria* and think only of drunkenness and a kind of poisoning that tilts the floor and turns our tongues into slippery toads. We should here think of inebriation as a flooding and a heightening, altering our perspectives, dulling our aches, quieting our fears, removing our inhibitions, increasing our jubilation, turning us into singers and joke-tellers and people thoroughly in love with the world.

The "*Anima Christi*" is never more human and charming than it is here. Holding onto the fact that Christ's *Calix Sanguinis mei* was a shared cup of paschal wine, the poet conjures whatever experience we have of intoxication in order to illustrate how the juice of grapes, poured into the blessing cup, can become the cup of Christ's precious blood in the great mystery of transubstantiation, and also how we can be substantially changed and enriched by drinking it. Christ's presence saves us but also uplifts us. We are not just to endure our short lives here in this God-begotten world, we are to enjoy them and rejoice in them.

Aqua lateris Christi, lava me.
"Water from the side of Christ, wash me."

• • •

In the passion narrative of the fourth gospel, we are told: "Then the soldiers came and broke the legs of the first and of the other who had been crucified with him. But when they came to Jesus and saw that he was already dead, they did not break his legs. Instead, one of the soldiers pierced his side with a spear, and at once blood and water flowed out." (Jn 19:32–34.)

We are intended to harken back to John's account of Jesus solemnly telling Nicodemus, the Pharisee who came to him by night, "Very truly, I tell you, no one can enter the kingdom of God without being born of water and Spirit," (Jn 3:5) or teaching the Samaritan woman at the well in Sychar, "Everyone who drinks of this water will be thirsty again, but those who drink of the water that I will give them will never be thirsty. The water that I will give will become in them a spring of water gushing up to eternal life." (Jn 4:13–14.)

Equally important to a precise reading of *lava me* is our awareness of the *Lavabo* and the priest's recital from Psalm 25 in the Tridentine Mass: "I wash my hands in innocence, and I go around Your altar, O Lord, giving voice to my thanks, and recounting all Your wondrous deeds . . . Gather not my soul with those of sinners, nor with men of blood my life. On their hands are crimes, and their right hands are full of bribes. But I walk in integrity; redeem me, and have pity on me."

Having been baptized and confirmed and having received holy communion, we are still in need of the rite of penance, of a cleansing from our sins and a reestablishment of a harmonious relationship with God; and Christ, through whom "God was pleased to reconcile to himself all things" (Col 1:20), is our perfect source and intercessor.

Passio Christi, conforta me.
"Passion of Christ, strengthen me."

I haven't paused on that word *passio* until reading it here in the context of *conforta*, which the centuries have turned into comfort and its associations of soothing and consolation and cheer. Looking up *passio*, I discovered its primary meaning was suffering or submission and only took on the English dictionary's definition of "the sufferings of Christ on the cross" because of one unexplained reference in Acts: "After his suffering he presented himself alive to them by many convincing proofs." (Acts 1:3.)

We think of passion as aroused or inflamed emotions, but Christ's passion was exactly otherwise, was one of obedience, humility, meekness, passivity, recollection, temperance, silence, and withdrawal. Without pose or trances or ecstasies, Christ passed the hours between his last supper and the crucifixion exactly like a contemplative at prayer. And that great lesson ought to both strengthen and comfort us, for Christ proved by his example that we defeat our distress and adversities by quietly submitting ourselves to God's will. Every hour should be blessed by Christ's final prayer: "Father, into your hands I commend my spirit." (Lk 23:46.)

• • •

O bone Jesu, exaudi me.
"O good Jesus, hear me."

Here the poet turns from Christological concepts to an affective appeal to the Jesus of Nazareth who likened himself to a good shepherd. And there is an irony in saying it, for Jesus hears us whenever we pray—his Godliness, his goodness, guarantees that. It is we who do not hear him or harden our hearts against him. But "hear me" needs saying if only to remind us that a great prayer does not require an "answer me," for that implies a reply in our own terms, in our own way. We handicap ourselves with human plans, but improve ourselves by being receptive to God.

Intra vulnera tua absconde me.
"Within your wounds hide me."

Again the Latin has a greater richness than the English, for *vulnera* means holes, injuries, infirmities, and misfortunes. We share with the human Jesus a host of vulnerabilities to hurts and criticisms and temptations. And he, having overcome them, has become both our guide and refuge. Hiding in his wounds is identical to *not* hiding in ours. We accept our human limitations while knowing that Christ's intercession makes it possible to triumph over them. And so we achieve the second meaning of *absconde me*, to stow away our infirmities, to leave ourselves behind.

• • •

Ne permittas me separari a te.
"Do not permit me to part from you."

We have been joined to Christ through baptism just as if we have been genetically fused or spliced or recombined. Complete separation from him results in our spiritual death, but the prayer here is talking as well about failings and turnings and equivocations. We should endeavor to conform to the example of Jesus, to be indistinguishable from him, for half measures have a way of leading to a greater difference. Hundreds of spiritual writers have issued precisely the same admonition—that whatever is alien to Christ is deleterious to us—but the author of "*Anima Christi*" seems more aware of our human propensity to desire or even demand a harmful disunion. Realizing our frailties and addictions, we forewarn our closest friend to not let us do what we will regret.

Ab hoste maligno defende me.
"From spiteful enemies protect me."

I have translated this line to underscore that the writer is not talking about a devil (*diabolus*) or demon (*daemon*) here, as a great many translations would have it, nor is the host, or army, as pernicious and hateful as enemies that are malignant in the English way. Every definition of *malignus* indicates pettiness and unkindness. A *hostis malignus* is stingy, ill-natured, grudging, small, the grouch next door, the snipe up the street, nothing so grand as an Evil One, nor even a *bête noire*. And I love that about the prayer.

Jacques Derrida has pointed out that our enemies are persons we haven't met yet; when we *have* met them, when we have done our best not to meet them and met them often and hour after hour, then our enemies are no more than *maligno* and too much like ourselves. How wise and practical of the "*Anima Christi*" to address the humdrum problems of Christianity rather than martyrdoms and persecutions: the frowns and jokes and put-downs, the belittlings and smirks.

In hora mortis meae voca me.
"In the hour of my death call me."

Hurrying toward the end of his prayer, the poet foresees the end of his earthly life and hopes that the "hear me" of four lines earlier is complemented by Christ's own call or summons. We are called throughout our lives to vocations of holiness, ministries, and activities on behalf of God and our communities, and even at the hour of our deaths we are called to find our fulfillment as human beings and as Christians.

Extreme unction and viaticum are hinted at in *hora mortis*. And from there on the "*Anima Christi*" floats with the freed and blessed anima of the writer as he jubilantly passes from this world to the next.

• • •

Et jube me venire ad te.
"And bid me to come to you."

Jube has the harsh meaning of an order or a command, but was also a Latin greeting at a door, as in "Enter." Nine lines of the prayer have been completed by the accusative pronoun *me*. But as the "*Anima Christi*" winds up, there is the "from you" of the eighth line and the "to you" of the eleventh, and the twelfth, penultimate line will have Christ's *te* without preposition, imitating Christ's shift to the central point in the writer's existence.

Ut cum sanctis tuis laudem te
"That with your saints I may praise you"

We move in our human lives from childhood's selfishness to maternal or paternal generosity and service. And so it is, and probably ought to be, in our spiritual life. We begin praying when we have urgent, if generally unimportant, needs and, when talking to God has become habitual, we gradually grow aware of our faults and our even more pressing need for forgiveness, until God's great mercies and goodness and faithfulness loom so hugely in our consciousness that we are in awe and whatever else we formerly did in prayer seems empty. Mystics often find intense gratification in merely being in the presence of the Holy One, their souls singing God's praise.

• • •

In saecula saeculorum. Amen.
"In the lifetime of lifetimes. So be it."

Knowing the medieval temper, we can presume without hazard that the poem's thirteen lines have reference to Christ and his twelve apostles. Eleven petitions represent the Eleven—the number of Christ's disciples after Judas Iscariot betrayed him and died. We recognize two general movements in the prayer: a chronological one from birth to death and from the initiation rites through holy communion and reconciliation to extreme unction and viaticum; and from rational, mystical, difficult constructions—*Anima Christi, sanctifica me*—through the affective and kataphatic—*Aqua lateris Christi, lava me*—to the common and pietistic—*In hora mortis meae voca me.* Every verb is Christ's but for the last, *laudem*, which interestingly extends for two lines, heralding a perpetual activity in the future.

Every important plea we can make is contained in our saying this brilliant prayer. Extolling and teaching, atoning and bidding, remembering and anticipating, the "*Anima Christi*" is complete both as a meditation and an appeal. Writing about the "Our Father," Simone Weil said that "It is to prayer what Christ is to humanity." Exactly the same thing can be said for this great prayer to Christ.

Stigmata

Rather late in my novel Mariette in Ecstasy, *Mother Saint-Raphaël speaks to the concerned nuns in the priory about Mariette's purported stigmata. "Wondrous things do happen here," the prioress says, "but they take place amidst great tranquillity. We shall make it our duty to preserve that. We shall try to find a natural explanation for these phenomena if we can, and we shall deny they are holy gifts to Mariette until there is no other alternative. We know there* are *miracles in the Gospels, but we show them disrespect if we dispose ourselves to believe in the simply fabulous. And we must keep in mind that there are a good many more pages in holy scripture that show how little pleasure God takes in astounding us with His power."*

My fictional character was speaking for me. Wondrous things do happen in life, but generally in the ordinary ways of faith and healing and love. Then there are phenomena like the stigmata for which there is no natural explanation and which seem so grossly old-fashioned, as misplaced in our modern times as witchcraft and sorcery. Mariette Baptiste was, for me, the real thing, a stigmatic; but I inserted an element of questionableness because in my research that seemed standard even in those instances in which the anomalies seemed authentic and all medical science could do was scratch its head in puzzlement.

A few years ago my friend Harold Fickett asked me to write about stigmata for his anthology Things in Heaven and Earth: Exploring the Supernatural. *It gave me the opportunity to provide some of the nonfiction background for the novel and to answer a few of the questions that readers often ask.*

Stigmata

At sunrise on the feast of the Holy Cross in 1224, a full month into a retreat of prayer and strict fasting, the forty-two-year-old Saint Francis of Assisi knelt outside his hut on Monte La Verna and fervently contemplated Christ's crucifixion. We read in the *Fioretti,* which records his life and sayings, that Saint Francis became so inflamed with love that he felt transformed into Jesus himself and saw a seraph with six fiery wings in front of him, bearing the form of a man nailed to a cross. At first he felt fright, then joy at seeing the face of Christ, who seemed so familiar to him and kindly, but when he viewed the nails in his hands and feet, Saint Francis was filled with infinite sorrow and compassion. Christ talked to him for a good while, about what we aren't told, after which

> this marvellous vision faded, leaving . . . in his body a wonderful image and imprint of the Passion of Christ. For in the hands and feet of Saint Francis forthwith began to appear the marks of the nails in the same manner as he had seen them in the body of Jesus crucified.

At first he tried to hide the five painful wounds—for his side, too, was pierced— but with his habit stained with blood and his feet so injured he could do no more than hobble, he was soon found out by the other friars with him, and he finally allowed them to look with awe on the wounds in his hands. On the back the flesh was raised and blackened in the form of the head of an iron spike, and in the torn palm the flesh looked like the point of a spike hammered flat.

We do not know, of course, if Saint Francis of Assisi was the first person to receive the stigmata—the word is a Latin derivation of the Greek for tattoo, scar, or mark—but he is the first to have that gift of Christ's wounds inspected and chronicled. Hundreds would have a comparable experience through the next seven centuries, generally getting the stigmata while in ecstasy, but in oddly differing ways.

Often, for example, their heads would bleed as from the Crown of Thorns, or mean welts would stripe their backs as if they'd been lashed forty times as Jesus was. While in a trance, Elizabeth of Herkenrode, a Belgian Cistercian nun, would strike herself on the jaw and roughly yank at her habit as if she were being hauled like Jesus from the house of Annas to the house of Caiaphas, and on to the praetorium. A farm girl in Brittany displayed in the flesh of her breast the words *O crux ave*, "hail, O cross." Theresa Neumann of Bavaria bled frighteningly from the eyes. She and many other stigmatics seem to have had fairly healthy lives with no food but the Holy Eucharist. Wounds to the hands and feet have been formed like nailheads on occasion, but also have been holes big enough for an examiner to read the page of a book through them. In Louise Lateau of Belgium, Saint Gemma Galgani of Italy, and, in 1972, the eleven-year-old Cloretta Robinson, a Baptist, blood would ooze up in their palms while being observed by physicians, but when the blood was wiped away, no laceration would ever be found. A few have been bruised on their right or left shoulder as if from carrying a heavy cross. And Christ's wound from the centurion's lance journeys in size and shape, between different ribs, or from side to side.

Women are seven times more likely than men to get the stigmata, and those in religious orders far outnumber all others who have received it. Age seems not to matter: An eight-year-old French girl has been given the wounds, and so has a sixty-five-year-old Sicilian nun. Occurrences of it are far more prevalent in Europe, and in particular Italy, than in other countries, and Catholicism is so typical in the phenomena that a stigmatic of another faith—there have been more than a few—is a genuine surprise.

Occasionally the stories of stigmata only fill one with pity. We read of a Mrs. H., a psychiatric patient in Australia, who claimed visions of Mary and wept tears of blood, but took her own life in 1963. Or Herr M., a businessman near Hamburg, a nominal Protestant who never went to church and whose stigmata were accompanied by intense headaches, confusion, and loss of weight, vision, and hearing. Saint Maria Maddalena de' Pazzi, a head-strong Carmelite nun in the sixteenth century, would tear off her habit and flamboyantly embrace a statue of Jesus while crying out in an orgasmic way, "O love, you are melting and dissolving my very being! You are consuming and killing me!" Aldous Huxley's history *The Devils of Loudun* relates the case of Sœur Jeanne des Anges, the prioress of an Ursuline convent, who, frustrated in love, first exhibited a bloody cross on her forehead, was publicly exorcised, and then, obviously craving more fame, became a florid spectacle throughout France as she flaunted the names of Jesus and the saints written in blood on her hand. And the Inquisition declared that Sor María de la Visitación faked her hand wounds with paint, having been induced to do so by two Dominican friars who wanted the "holy nun of Lisbon" to augur hell for the king of Portugal unless he fulfilled their wishes.

Reviewing the Roman Catholic Church's hundreds of investigations of stigmata in our far more skeptical age, it's quite easy to find hoaxes, delusions, misinterpretations, and a host of theatrical, masochistic neurotics, or sincere people who have fallen prey to a forlorn and fraudulent piety. And it's a fact that only in a few instances has the Church ever ruled an occurrence of stigmata to be genuine, even then encouraging a variety of causes and extenuations, none of which have anything to do with the supernatural.

In Germany, in 1928, when the thirty-year-old Therese Neumann was attracting international attention with Christ's bloody wounds, with a lifelong fast that included no food beyond the communion Host, and with visions in which she talked to Jesus in Aramaic, a language she could not have known, Doktor Alfred Lechler, a psychiatrist, took into his consultation a mentally ill twenty-six-year-old woman whom he called Elizabeth K. Working in his house as a maid, she was available for continual observation and hypnotic suggestion, and Lechler found it irresistible to try to have Elizabeth K. imitate Therese Neumann's feats. While she was in a trance, the psychiatrist told Elizabeth that nails were being hammered into her hands and feet, and the next day, he said, she manifested red and swollen abrasions. She was shown magazine photographs of blood welling from Therese's eyes, and within hours she was shedding bloodstained tears. Elizabeth K. even went without food for a week and, through Lechler's hypnosis, managed to gain weight.

Of course, the fact that functions and symptoms can be replicated does not mean they have fundamentally the same source, and there is a world of difference between the fraught and uneasy lives of psychotics like Mrs. H. and Elizabeth K. and the health and serenity of those stigmatics whose holiness was the conduit for wonders.

Look, for example, at the famous Italian mystic Francesco

Forgione, who took the name Pio after entering the Capuchin order of the Franciscans at the age of fifteen. Ordained a priest in 1910, and forced to serve as a medical orderly during World War I, Padre Pio finally took up residence in the friary of Santa Maria delle Grazie in the village of San Giovanni Rotondo on the Adriatic Sea. There, on September 20, 1918, he was sitting in choir making his postcommunion thanksgiving when he saw a heavenly light containing the form of Christ on the cross. Shafts of flame from the cross pierced his hands and feet, and, he wrote his father guardian, the Capuchin superior:

> I was suddenly filled with great peace and abandonment which effaced everything else and caused a lull in the turmoil. All this happened in a flash. Meanwhile I saw before me a mysterious person . . . his hands and feet and side were dripping blood. The sight frightened me, and what I felt at that moment cannot be described. I thought I should die, and indeed I should have died if the Lord had not intervened and strengthened my heart, which was about to burst out of my chest.
>
> The vision disappeared and I became aware that my own hands and feet and side were dripping blood. Imagine the agony I experienced and continue to experience almost every day. The heart wound bleeds continually, especially from Thursday evening until Saturday. Dear Father, I am dying of pain because of the wound and the resulting embarrassment. I am afraid I shall bleed to death if the Lord does not hear my heartfelt supplication to relieve me of this condition.

The afflictions never healed, were never infected, and Padre Pio was soon famous. Hundreds of the faithful would line up to have him hear their confessions, or fill the pews for his Masses just to receive communion from his bleeding and half-mittened hands. Eminent physicians confirmed the authenticity of his wounds, but a wary Pope Pius XI—acting on misinformation, he later said—effectively imprisoned Padre Pio within the friary while the Church investigated the stigmata, a harassment that would continue off and on throughout his life. And his reputation only increased.

Whole books have been filled with tales of his holiness and miracles during the fifty years of his stigmata. Wild dogs were reported to visit the friary during his Mass, quietly listen to his voice, and at the *Ite, missa est* trot away. Mass with him would last three or four hours, so often did he fall into ecstasy in it, and he heard the thoughts of his congregation, offering their fears and prayers with his own. A hefty man, his only food was a few vegetables and a pittance of fish at midday, no more than three hundred calories. To a friend he confessed that the excruciating pain he constantly felt was only magnified if he slept, and so he did not sleep but prayed. Many claimed he was favored with the odor of sanctity, and wherever he went one could smell the exquisite perfume of a spice like cumin.

His was a gruff saintliness: He scowled at idiocies, chided whiners, hated television, brusquely answered most questions before they were asked, hotly refused to forgive sins that he knew were already confessed and forgiven, foresaw the future, fought with demons, healed people through touch, through ghostly visitations, through their dreams.

A teenaged girl with one leg in a thigh-high cast was horrified to find that her toes had turned black. Doctors feared she'd contracted gangrene and would have to have the leg amputated. She appealed to Padre Pio for help and he touched the cast; and when the hospital removed the hard plaster in preparation for surgery, the doctors were shocked to see that the formerly injured leg was fully healed and more beautiful than the other.

A baby girl was born who was such a grotesque and twisted mass of flesh that doctors didn't know how to begin treating her. Signora Roversi, the mother, took the infant to church and dumped her in Padre Pio's lap, firmly insisting she wouldn't leave until the child was cured. The girl grew up to be as supple and tall as an Amazon.

Humiliated on the field of battle, an Italian general was about to kill himself with his revolver when a friar suddenly appeared in his tent and shouted, "What on earth do you think you're doing?" The friar gently counseled him until the general agreed to live out his full life, but when the friar left, the general went out and upbraided his sentry for letting a priest get past him. And he was flabbergasted to hear than no one had gone in or out. Much later, of course, he would find out that the friar was Padre Pio.

A farmer in Padua, three hundred miles north of the friary,

was ailing with occlusions to the blood vessels in his lungs that no medical treatment could cure. Realizing he was dying, the farmer prayed for intercession and was surprised by a friendly apparition of a bearded friar who laid his hand on the farmer's chest, smiled, and disappeared. Completely healed, but so embarrassed by the weird circumstances that he told no one but his mother about them, the farmer went to a lunch months later and was amazed to find hanging on the wall of the house a photograph of a friar he thought was imaginary. That night he journeyed south by train to San Giovanni Rotondo, to offer his gratitude to Padre Pio who, after hearing the farmer's sins in confession, asked quite naturally, "And tell me, what about the lungs now? How are they?"

In World War II an American Army Air Corps squadron leader disobeyed the order to bomb San Giovanni Rotondo because he saw the gigantic form of a friar in the sky, fiercely diverting the aircraft, and was chagrined to have to write that in an official report. Worried that he had lost his faculties, the pilot found out about Padre Pio through offhand inquiries, and after the war visited Santa Maria delle Grazie, becoming one of Pio's "children."

One night the friars were awakened by hundreds of voices happily cheering Padre Pio, but when they looked in the hallways, no one was there. A friend asked Pio about it later and was frankly told those were the souls in purgatory thanking him for his prayers.

Often he blessed holy gifts and, in a country of faulty mail service, packages, but once, shouting in wild anger, he forced a man to open a beautifully wrapped box. The friar then flung out its contents of books, holy pictures, and rosaries until he found hidden in the bottom a handful of lottery tickets. Tearing them into confetti, he thundered to his flock, "Get out! Get out! Devils, all of you!"

There is a story that Karol Wojtyla, the bishop of Craców, visited the friary in 1962 and in a letter written in Latin later requested healing for a mother of six who was dying of cancer. Padre Pio wrote back, saying the mother was free of the illness and as a postscript noted that the Polish bishop would be the pontiff someday. Karol Wojtyla would be ordained Pope John Paul II in 1978, ten years after Padre Pio's death.

In 1995, nearly thirty years after Padre Pio's death, a two-and-a-half-year-old cancer patient named Michael Ortega was left overnight in a San Jose, California, hospital as he awaited a bone marrow transplant. Jackie Ortega, his mother, told my sister's niece that it was the first time Michael had been away from his family, so the next morning she wondered how he'd done on his own. The boy told her he was fine, that a man in a beard and a brown robe had entertained him until late by playing piano for him. She naturally thought Michael had been dreaming. A few weeks later she was given a book on Padre Pio by a friend, and was holding it as she visited Michael. The boy smiled at the book jacket and said, "That's him! That's the man who's been visiting me!"

A friar companion said of him:

> He was living in another dimension, with one foot here and the other in the supernatural world. He maintained a perfect balance, and never let you know what was going on. One day, in this very hall, a woman whose son had recently died came up to him. She said, "Padre, please tell me if my son is in heaven." And he flashed back, as sharp as ever, "Why, yes, I've just come from there myself, this very moment."

A fool once told the friar that his wounds were caused by focusing too much on Christ's crucifixion. To which Padre Pio hotly suggested, "Go out in a field and stare at a bull and see if you grow horns."

Questions and requests of all kinds were brought to Padre Pio by the villagers of San Giovanni Rotondo: whether to buy a car, sell a home, change jobs, take as a husband this man, give away this favorite rosary. Will you heal my wife's tumor? Will you give my old mother just one more year? Won't you please make Papa quit the Communist Party? When will I fall in love?

Would he have become so famous, so necessary, were it not for his stigmata? Was it not a sign that attracted the faithful to him, who himself was a further sign of God's fatherly concern for the humblest things that trouble us?

In *Mariette in Ecstasy* I told the story of a passionate and attractive seventeen-year-old who in 1906 joins the religious order of the Sisters of the Crucifixion in upstate New York. At

Christmas, the postulant's older sister, the convent's prioress, dies of cancer, and soon after the funeral Mariette Baptiste is favored with Christ's wounds. An investigation is begun within the convent of Our Lady of Sorrows to find out whether Mariette is the real thing, or a schemer full of trickery, or a madwoman confusing sexual yearning with religious ecstasy.

Mother Saint-Raphaël, the new prioress, is troubled by the stigmata not only because Mariette's fame is hurting the tranquillity of the cloister, but also because she can't understand why God would give Christ's wounds in such a way. Confronting the postulant in her infirmary bed, Mother Saint-Raphaël says, "'I see no possible reasons for it.'"

> "Is it so Mariette Baptiste will be praised and esteemed by the pious? Or is it so she shall be humiliated and jeered at by skeptics? Is it to honor religion or humble science? And what are these horrible wounds, really? A trick of anatomy, a bleeding challenge to medical diagnosis, a brief and baffling injury that hasn't yet, in six hundred years, changed our theology or our religious practices. Have you any idea how disruptive you've been? You are awakening hollow talk and half-formed opinions that have no place in our priory, and I have no idea why God would be doing this to us. To you. I do know that the things the villagers have been giving us have not helped us in our vow of poverty. And all the seeking people who have been showing up have not helped our rule of enclosure. And there are breaches to our vow of obedience whenever you become the topic."
>
> She sees that the postulant is staring at her impassively,

with a hint, even, of amusement. She says in a sterner way, "I flatter myself that I have been extremely tolerant and patient, thus far. I have done so out of respect for your late sister, and in sympathy for the torment you have in her loss. But I shall not suffer your confusions much longer. And so I pray, Mariette, that if it is in your power to stop this—as I presume it is—that you do indeed stop it." She pauses and then stands. "And if it is in your power to heal me of the hate and envy I have for you now, please do that as well."

If the fruits of stigmata are truly the esteem of the pious, hollow talk, confusion, hate, and envy, one may indeed wonder why God would grace the world with them. I do have some possible reasons for it. We are so far away from the Jesus of history that he can seem a fiction, a myth—the greatest story ever told, but no more. We have a hint of his reality, and the shame and agony of his Crucifixion, in those whom God has graced with stigmata. Conversions of life have come from them. We are taught the efficacy of prayer, the joy that can be found even in suffering, and the enormous, untapped powers of the human body and mind. That some who have been given them are irreligious only confirms the fact that they are favors freely given, not earned. That such a high proportion of stigmatics are women may be God's way of illustrating the importance of women in Christ's ministry and of correcting the imbalance in Holy Scripture, where a far higher proportion of men have their voices heard.

Cynics may find in stigmata only wish fulfillment, illness, or fakery, but the faithful ought to find in them vibrant and disturbing symbols of Christ's Incarnation and his painful, redemptive death on the cross.

I think of an English biochemist named Cecil who was in Italy when he fell asleep at the wheel of his car and woke up in a hospital, floating near death, his arms, legs, ribs, and skull fractured. A Franciscan friar walked into his room, forced him to confess his sins, gave him communion and last rites, and went away. Like others, Cecil would find out the friar was Padre Pio. Later, he visited Santa Maria delle Grazie and while the old friar celebrated Mass, Cecil felt transported to Calvary, as if he were really present at the Crucifixion. "I was utterly overcome," the Englishman said.

"Padre Pio made me visualize Christ's agony in the garden, with all its horror and revulsion. . . . He made me understand the extent of the pain and anguish, the price of sin and of saving souls. He showed me what the Crucifixion cost God—as far as any human being can grasp its magnitude."

We cannot grasp that magnitude, so it may be that God on occasion grants us witnesses.

Hearing the Cry of the Poor: The Jesuit Martyrs of El Salvador

Susan Bergman contacted me in 1994 about a book she was editing and wanted me to contribute to. She was then thinking of calling it A Cloud of Witnesses, *from the metaphor for the Christian faithful in the "Letter to the Hebrews" of the first century, and in it she wanted contemporary writers to consider those men and women in the twentieth century who chose to stand by their faith and its commitment to justice at the cost of their lives.*

The book was published in 1996 under the title Martyrs, *and in it twenty writers presented a stunning indictment of the last century's vast and sustained persecution of religious belief: Dietrich Bonhoeffer in Hitler's Germany, Osip Mandlestam in Stalin's Russia, Archbishop Oscar Romero in El Salvador, Charles de Foucauld in Algeria, Steven Biko in South Africa, Janani Luwum in Uganda, and the stories of Christian missionaries in China and Ecuador.*

My colleagues in the faculty and administration of Santa Clara

University were friends of the six Jesuit priests who were murdered by Salvadoran soldiers in 1989, and from one of them I heard a story that will serve as my prologue: A few weeks after the cold-blooded assassinations of November 16, an American Jesuit visited the hillside residence where the murders occurred. The house interior had been torn apart by the soldiers, chunks of wall were shot out by stray bullets, wherever he looked there were signs of wreckage and violence, and yet as he paused in a hallway he was suddenly overcome with a feeling of immense and surprising joy. Whatever anger, despair, and sadness he was feeling gave way to a mysterious happiness and peace. The American just stood there for a moment, fully absorbing it, and then he noticed in the hallway an older Jesuit resident who smiled as he walked past and simply said, "I see you have found the spot."

Hearing the Cry of the Poor: The Jesuit Martyrs of El Salvador

In the fall of 1989, the Jesuit theologian Jon Sobrino was teaching a brief course in Christology in Thailand when a fellow priest awakened him one night with the news that a Jesuit had been killed in El Salvador. The Irish priest said he'd only half-heard it on the BBC's World Service radio broadcast so for further information he'd phoned London and Julian Filochowski, the director of an international aid agency and a good friend of the Central American Jesuits. Filochowski, hearing that Sobrino was presently there in Hua Hin, asked to speak to him directly.

Walking to the phone, Sobrino feared the news concerned his friend Ignacio Ellacuría, the well-known and frequently threatened rector of the University of Central America in San Salvador. And so when Filochowski told him, "Something terrible has happened," Sobrino at once said, "I know. Ellacuría." But he did not know. His friend told him that Ellacuría indeed had been killed, and then he went on. Also killed were Ignacio Martín-Baró, Segundo Montes, Juan Ramón Moreno, Amando López, and Joaquin López y López. Even a cook, Elba Ramos, and her sixteen-year-old daughter, Celina.

"My friend read the names slowly," Sobrino remembered, "and each of them reverberated like a hammer blow that I received in total helplessness. I was writing them down, hoping that the list would end after each name. But after each name came another, on to the end. The whole community, my whole community, had been murdered."

Ignacio Ellacuría had celebrated his fifty-ninth birthday just a week before his murder. He was born in the Basque region of Spain—as was Saint Ignatius, the founder of the Society of Jesus—and was the fourth of five boys in his family to go into religious life, entering the Jesuit novitiate in Loyola in 1947. Encouraged to be a missionary by Miguel Elizondo, the novice master who would instruct, or "form," five of the six martyred Jesuits, young Ellacuría went to El Salvador with six others in 1949 in order to found a new novitiate in the vice-province of

Central America—comprised of Costa Rica, El Salvador, Guatemala, Nicaragua, and Panama. (Forty years later, a columnist for *Diario de Hoy* wrote of Ellacuría that shortly "after World War II, a sinister person arrived in the country, and it wouldn't be much of a surprise if he turned out to be a KGB agent.")

After five years of humanities, classical languages, and philosophy at the Catholic University in Quito, Ecuador, Ellacuría returned to San Salvador for his three-year regency, teaching in a high school seminary. Then he was sent to Innsbruck, Austria, for four years of theology, having as one of his Jesuit professors there the formidable and influential Karl Rahner, one of the principal architects of the *aggiornamento*, or updating, of the Catholic Church in the Second Vatican Council.

Ellacu, as he was called by his friends, was unhappy in Austria. While he was the acknowledged leader of his Hispanic peers, he was perceived by his father superiors less favorably, as an intense, imperative, lofty man with fierce magnetism and often forbidding intellect. A Jesuit examiner wrote of him: "While he is highly talented, his character is one that is potentially difficult; his own spirit of critical judgment is persistent and not open to others; he separates himself from the community in small groups amongst whom he exercises a strong influence."

Ellacuría was ordained in 1961 and, following a fourth year of theology in Austria, commenced work on his doctorate in philosophy at the University of Madrid, writing his dissertation on the Spanish philosopher Xavier Zubiri, a theoretician of popular political movements whose work investigated, as Ellacuría later put it, "the truth of what seemed to him to be the fundamentals in human life." At last, in 1967, nine years after he left for theological studies, Ellacuría returned to San Salvador to teach philosophy at the *Universidad Centroamericana José Simeón Cañas*—named after a nineteenth-century Salvadoran priest who fought for the abolition of slavery—which was then little more than a handful of courses and a fifth year of high school.

The University of Central America had been funded in 1964 by wealthy parents, politicians, and a Catholic Church hierarchy that wanted an antidote to the toxic Marxism that was poisoning education at the federally run National University. Without a site or financial foundation, with only a few fervent Jesuits, secretaries, and faculty members who taught for free as a favor to the fathers, the University of Central America at first relied solely on the high repute of the Society of Jesus for its prestige and seriousness. But that was enough. Within a few years a sloping, coffee-growing plantation in the hills south of the city had given rise to a palmy campus that housed highly regarded faculties in industrial engineering and economics, finally enrolling seven thousand students who were generally from Salvadoran high society, financially privileged young men and women who, it was thought, would use their advantages to help the less fortunate.

Ellacuría, who was put on the university's five-man board of directors, found that premise troubling. While the institution's orientation was formally that of providing technicians for the economic and social development of El Salvador, he thought it was essentially affirming European values and structures, and fostering prosperity for the prosperous. Ellacuría felt the institution ought to fully engage the harsh realities of the Third World and, through teaching, research, and persuasion, be a voice for those who have no voice, to alter or annihilate the world's inhuman and unjust structures, and help assuage the agony of the poor. With his forceful guidance and his editing of the monthly magazine, *Estudios Centroamericanos*, the University of Central America would undergo an epistemological shift, orienting its ethos in the fundamental option for the poor and in the liberation theology formulated by Gustavo Gutiérrez, a theology founded on life in the risen Christ while it was focused on the institutions of injustice and death to which Latin America's poor were subjected.

There was much to do. El Salvador was a tiny country—about the size of Israel, or New Jersey—but with five million people had the greatest population density in the Western Hemisphere. Coffee had created El Salvador's foreign exchange, financed its public works, furnished jobs to its wage-earners, and bestowed huge fortunes on fourteen families that had formed an oligarchy in what was still a feudal society. El Salvador did not fit well into the First and Second World models of a free market, trickle down, privatized economy, for the wealthy had persisted in holding onto a fierce capitalism that went far beyond avarice. Eight percent of the population owned 50 percent of the gross national product, while 92 percent fought to find a fragile subsistence on what was left over, getting by, or not, on an average income of $141 per year. Half the children did not finish primary school. Two percent of the population owned cars. Life for the landless majority was one of rootlessness, wattle huts, filth and illness, and half-mile walks to fetch contaminated water in a bucket, hunger forever there with them like a dog at heel. Wish for and want may have been the only necessary verbs.

> And he came to Nazareth, where he had been brought up; and he went to the synagogue, as his custom was, on the Sabbath day. And he stood up to read; and there was given to him the book of the prophet Isaiah. He opened the book and found the place where it was written,
>
> "The Spirit of the Lord is upon me, because he has anointed me to preach good news to the poor.
> He has sent me to proclaim release to the captives and recovering of sight to the blind, to set at liberty those who are oppressed, to proclaim the acceptable year of the Lord."
>
> (Lk 4:16–19)

Ellacuría once argued that priesthood and religious life found its meaning in the Third World, for there the professed vows of poverty, chastity, and obedience offered a liberating freedom from First World values of wealth, hedonism, and power. At a disputatious retreat for Central American Jesuits, Ellacuría spoke compellingly of the sin of the province to which he belonged, saying the Society of Jesus had collaborated in shoring up unjust structures and oppression in the Third World by favoring the rich with their schools and ministries in the past, and in the future would need to concentrate on liberating the poor from sin, hunger, ignorance, misery, and persecution.

Older Jesuits felt their hard efforts were being nullified, but Jesuits still in formation felt inspired to take a far more activist role in countering injustice, some of them joining Salvadoran Jesuit Rutilio Grande and his pastoral "accompaniment" of the *campesinos* in the parish of Aguilares. These seminarians were firebrands in their late twenties and thirties from well-to-do families, for whom Third World poverty became a harsh reality for the first time. They'd study books like Jon Sobrino's *The Historical Jesus* at the Center for Theological Reflection founded by Ellacuría and Sobrino, and then go out to the parish, where they'd see at firsthand a crucified people. A few scholastics began to feel a stronger call to organizing a popular revolutionary movement than to studies for the priesthood, a neglect that Ellacuría criticized for he felt that academic studies free from ideology or the encumbrance of politics would be more valuable in analyzing and correcting the conditions of the 40 percent of Salvadorans who lived in dire poverty.

Unfortunately, three Jesuit seminarians left the order to take up arms against the so-called national security forces that were wreaking vengeance on those nuns and priests and Protestant missionaries who'd allied themselves with the poor. Soon the presence of a New Testament in a house was enough to have that house destroyed by the police. Whole villages were wiped out. Writer and television producer Teresa Whitfield wrote that after the 1979 Young Officers' coup, which brought in a civilian-military junta, "El Salvador had hit and held the international headlines as a Central American hellhole where death squads ran riot, unarmed *campesinos* were slaughtered by the score, and unidentified bodies, or parts of them, turned up on the roadside each morning."

Rutilio Grande was also one of those that *los escuadrones de la muerte* [death squads] sought out. In the parish of Aguilares, Father Grande and his team of three priests officiated at formal religious functions and furnished pastoral care as before, but they also worked to form a tightly knit community of brothers and sisters in Christ that could fashion a new world. Within a short time three hundred people there were committed to the ministry of the Word, coordinating liturgies and catechism classes, and stressing the Gospel message that God's will was the building of a Kingdom of heaven on earth.

Then the wealthy owner of a sugar plantation in Aguilares was killed outside his estate while, coincidentally, the ordination of three Jesuit priests was being celebrated by the archbishop, forty Jesuits, and two thousand *campesinos*—who were soon being called "hordes of assassins." Again the Latin American Society of Jesus was accused of favoring the rebels and fostering subversion.

A presidential candidate promised to rid El Salvador of the Jesuits within three months of his election. The Committee for the Defense of the Fatherland, the Catholic Association of Mothers, and other government front organizations found their greatest enemies were not hunger and misery but liberation theology and its Jesuit teachers. Ellacuría was among those priests exiled from El Salvador for a time; other foreigners were interrogated with torture or expelled, including a Colombian priest from the parish next to Aguilares for whom Rutilio Grande filled in at a Mass. In his homily Grande said, "I greatly fear, my brothers, that very soon the Bible and the Gospel will not be allowed within our country. We'll get the covers and nothing more, because all its pages are subversive. . . . And I fear, my brothers, that if Jesus of Nazareth returned . . . they would arrest him. They would take him to the courts and accuse him of being unconstitutional and subversive."

On the afternoon of March 12, 1977, Rutilio Grande got into his white Jeep with an old man, Manuel Solórzano, a fifteen-year-old boy named Nelson Rutilio, and three children, and headed for a Mass in the village of El Paisnal, where Rutilio had been born forty-nine years earlier. Waylaid by heavily armed soldiers on his right and left in the sugar cane fields, Father Grande was heard to quietly say, "We must do as God wills," and then he and the old man and boy were coldbloodedly killed. The children in back of the Jeep got away.

Late that night Archbishop Oscar Romero con-celebrated a Mass for the dead in Aguilares, and afterwards humbly begged the gathered priests and nuns to tell him what the Church ought to do next. The Jesuits there were surprised. Although he'd been educated by them in San Salvador and at the Gregorian University in Rome, Monsignor Romero had not been friendly to the Society of Jesus in El Salvador, having gotten its men removed from the faculty of the National Seminary, having warned a pontifical commission about their politicization of the clergy, and having been a longtime follower of the highly conservative *Opus Dei* movement. And he was hampered, too, by the fact that when the papal nuncio consulted wealthy businessmen and government officials about their choice for the archdiocese, he was the one preferred.

Either they'd got him wrong or he was changed by the office or by grace, for from the time of Rutilio Grande's murder Oscar Romero was a different man, offending the right-wing press, the papal nuncio, his fellow bishops, and those in high society who'd thought he was one of them. And now his friends and allies were the same Jesuits held in contempt by those in power. Soon Romero's press secretary, the president of the governing board of the archdiocese, the general manager of its radio station, his consultors and writers, even his confessor were all Jesuits. And Romero inspired them with his evangelization of the culture and his serenity, prayerfulness, and fortitude in the face of evil, giving the university a greater consciousness of its own Christian mission in the Third World. Ellacuría would say of him, "With Monsignor Romero, God passed through El Salvador."

Leaflets had been floating around San Salvador that read: "*Haga patria, mate un Cura!*" "Be a patriot, kill a priest!" Eleven would be killed between 1977 and 1980, but also killed were four North American churchwomen, and Lutheran, Episcopalian, Mennonite, and Baptist missionaries—any of those who imitated Christ in opting for the poor. And yet they stayed on. "We have not remained because we are obstinate," the Jesuit provincial wrote, "but because we are thinking of our brothers, especially the dispossessed, who have suffered more than we . . . . We have remained to make a small testimony to the loyalty of the church."

Archbishop Romero said in a homily, "I am glad, brothers and sisters, that they have murdered priests in this country, because it would be very sad if in a country where they are murdering the people so horrifically, there were no priests among the victims. It is a sign that the church has become truly incarnate in the problems of the people."

Ellacuría was with him when he planned his homily for March 23, 1980. Romero would talk about the fifth commandment and the thousands who were being slaughtered, and he would implore the soldiers and police to heed God's law, not the godless commands of their superiors. "In the name of God,"

Romero said, "and in the name of this suffering people whose cries rise up to the heavens every day more tumultuously, I beg you, I beseech you, I order you in the name of God: Stop the repression!" Early in the evening of the following day, while he was celebrating Mass in a hospital chapel, preparing the gifts for the Offertory, a national policeman walked in, shot Archbishop Romero through the heart, and hurried out.

Of course the government offered its condolences and there was an official investigation of the murder, but over twenty years have passed and no one has been charged with the crime.

> **What does it profit, my brethren, if a man says he has faith but has not works? Can his faith save him? If a brother or sister is ill-clad and in lack of daily food, and one of you says to them, "Go in peace, be warmed and filled," without giving them the things needed for the body, what does it profit? So faith by itself, if it has no works, is dead. (Jas 2:14–17)**

Archbishop Romero had walked through a door that he'd left open for his Jesuit friends. In 1979 Ignacio Ellacuría had been named rector, or president, of the University of Central America and became a far more public man. Two years later Ignacio Martín-Baró was named academic vice-rector, Ellacuría's right-hand man.

Twelve years younger than his friend, Ellacu, Ignacio Martín-

Baró, or Nacho as he was called, was born in Valladolid, Spain, in 1942. In formation he was thought to be hugely talented but too serious and intense, an uptight perfectionist whom his Jesuit classmates finally humanized to such an extent that friends later characterized Nacho as a "boon companion." While studying humanities and philosophy in Bogotá, Colombia, Martín-Baró became engrossed by psychology and filled his nights reading whatever books on it he could find. Right after his ordination to the priesthood, he was assigned to the University of Central America, where he taught psychology and was a popular dean of students until he left for the University of Chicago, where he was awarded a Ph.D. in social psychology in 1979, with a dissertation on population density in El Salvador.

With his *norte americano* colleagues, Martín-Baró often wise-cracked, "In your country, it's publish or perish. In ours, it's publish *and* perish." And publish he did, writing frequently for Ellacuría's *Estudios Centroamericanos* on a wide variety of subjects, whether it was the latest Nobel Prize for literature or Latin American *machismo* or the problems of marijuana use. Chair of the psychology department at UCA, vice rector, a member of the five-man board of directors, and founder of the Institute of Public Opinion, which did polling and canvassing of the people to counteract the government-controlled media's "public disinformation"—Martín-Baró was of necessity a workaholic, getting to his office before six A.M. and generally staying until eight P.M., and often following formal meetings with late-night chat sessions at which he'd sing and play guitar. Weekends he spent in a parish in Jayaque, where he left behind his harried, intellectual life to become "Padre Nacho," his trouser pockets full of candies for the children, his face lighting up with love and joy as he ministered and preached to his congregation. "A Cervantes with his pen or at the computer," as a friend described him, "as an orator he could have captivated an auditorium of the deaf."

Martín-Baró was internationally famous for a psychology of liberation that eschewed Western scientism, ahistoricism, and self-centered individualism in order to orient psychology toward service to communities and to the rights of workers, *campesinos*, union organizers, and mothers of the "disappeared."

Writing in the *International Journal of Mental Health*, Martín-Baró pointed out that the Reagan-Bush White House pretended that El Salvador was premier among the Latin American democracies, having, as it seemed, a government chosen in free elections, an ever-increasing respect for human rights, and a highly professional army under civilian control. What few problems there were in the functioning of the judicial system, the White House proposed, were in fact fomented by Marxist-Leninist terrorists.

The hard realities were far different. Civil war had brought not only violence, polarization, and the "institutionalized lie" to El Salvador, but also psychological trauma that would have far-reaching effects on a whole generation. Looking at a tiny village used as a hiding place by the insurgents of the Farabundo

Martí National Liberation Front (FMLN) and periodically wiped out by the Salvadoran armed forces solely for that reason, he found that whenever even a far-off military operation was begun, "the people take shelter in their houses gripped by a series of psychosomatic symptoms: generalized trembling of the body, muscular weakness, diarrhea." His field workers collected "clear evidence that government soldiers practice systematic sexual abuse of the *campesina* women," and found that *campesinos* were afraid to even talk about the civil war. Even when they were shown crops that had been put to flame or houses that were pockmarked with bullet holes, the frightened farmers insisted on their ignorance of the cause, saying that the damage must have happened when they were away from home. And when children from the higher economic sectors were asked what would have to happen for there to be no more poor people, a few answered, "Kill them all."

Working in much the same areas as Martín-Baró was Segundo Montes, who was famous both in El Salvador and the United States for his analysis of exiles, refugees, and the displaced. Like Ellacuría and Martín-Baró, he was punishingly overworked: he was the religious superior of the Jesuit community—often a full-time job at other universities—as well as the chair of the departments of sociology and political science, one of the five on the board of directors, the head of the Human Rights Institute, and a weekend pastor at a parish in Santa Tecla.

A tall, majestic, passionate Spaniard with a fierce scowl and beard, Segundo Montes was called Zeus by his students, for whom he had a fatherly affection. Educated initially in the hard sciences, he taught physics at the Jesuit high school in San Salvador—the *Externado San José*—during his regency, and after his Austrian theology studies and ordination he went back to be prefect of discipline and headmaster there. But he saw he could do far more good as a social analyst than as a physicist, so he went on to get a doctorate in anthropology at the University of Madrid and fulfilled his former penchant for numbers with statistics.

Researching subjects as varied as land holdings, social stratification, patronage, and the pervasive theft of dollars mailed from workers in the United States to their Salvadoran families, Montes stirred up as many enemies as Ellacuría had. In 1980 a high-powered bomb exploded at the foot of his bed in the old Jesuit house on Calle Mediterráneo, blowing out a hole in the floor the size of a trash can lid. On another night he and Ellacuría left a dinner and found their little white car painted with blood-red swastikas and slogans, including DEATH TO THE COMMUNISTS OF THE UCA! And in the early 1980s he heard from army officers who'd formerly been his high school students that there was a plan to murder Ellacuría first and then himself and the three other men who directed the university. Segundo Montes shrugged and told a worried staff member, "What am I going to do? If they kill me, they kill me." When a journalist asked in 1988 if he'd thought about seeking freedom elsewhere, Montes told him, "We here are not just teachers and social scientists. We are also parish priests, and the people need to have the Church stay with them in these terrible times—the rich as well as the poor. The rich need to hear from us, just as do the poor. God's grace does not leave, so neither can we."

The fourth member of the board at the University of Central America was the Spaniard Juan Ramón Moreno, who was born in 1933 and was known to his friends as Pardito. A highly intelligent, haltingly shy and sensitive man, his first assignment as a regent was biology classes in the high school of the San Salvador seminary where Ellacuría taught, but besides some work in bioethics, that was as far as he went with his great love of science, and he failed to get a doctorate or even a master's degree in any field, a humiliating oddity among Jesuit priests. Moreno held a host of jobs in vice-province service and formation, having been a novice master, a teacher in the juniorate, a province consultor, a secretary to the provincial, an editor of the province newsletter, and a spiritual director for a great number of sisters and priests in religious orders throughout Latin America.

Ever tactful and self-effacing, Moreno was named interim rector of San Salvador's *Externado San José* in 1972 in order to investigate charges by high society parents that their sons and daughters were having their heads filled with talk of the class struggle and then going on field trips among El Salvador's poor, after which they were angrily denouncing their families for being bourgeois, as if it were criminal to strive for economic well-being. Looking carefully into the matter, Moreno found out that the high school students were not reading Marxist tracts but papal encyclicals, and that they were shocked because the injustice and poverty were shocking. Quiet rationality was not what was wanted, however, and the progovernment newspaper *Prensa Gráfica* hounded Moreno out of office with fulminations about him wrapping Christ and the Gospels in Communism.

The founder in Panama of a magazine for religious called *Diakonia*, which in Greek means "service," in the 1980s Moreno brought the publication and its library with him to the University of Central America, where he was librarian for the Center for Theological Reflection and assistant director of the new Oscar Romero Center. There, on the night of his martyrdom, in wanton retribution for his crimes of thoughtfulness and conscientious administration, soldiers would firebomb his filing cabinets and wipe out the hard disks on the computers he'd installed.

In the 1970s, when Juan Rámon Moreno was assisting in a nationwide literacy campaign in Nicaragua, Amando López was one of his superiors. López was then head of the Central American University in Managua, having moved there from the post of rector at the *Colegio Centro América*. Amando López was born in Spain in 1936, studied in Rome, got his doctorate in theology at Strasbourg in 1970, and, at age thirty-four, was put in charge of San Salvador's diocesan seminary. Within no time the bishops who'd been impressed by his credentials were woefully disappointed. Expecting López to form the seminarians as they themselves had been formed, the prelates were offended at finding out that López was instituting changes that were prompted by Vatican II: the faculty were far less aloof, regulations were far less intrusive, soccer was now being played inside the walls, old-fashioned cassocks were being discarded, and the seminarians were going over to the UCA to get their philosophy classes from that wild man Ellacuría. In 1972, after heated deliberations, López and the full faculty of Jesuits were fired from their jobs.

López had taught at the high school in Managua as a scholastic, so it was a good fit for him to be assigned as rector there, and then at the Central American University of Nicaragua after the Sandinista revolution. The United States Congress was up to then following the urgings of the White House in financing the governments of infamous autocrats like Anastasio Somoza and the shah of Iran if that meant fending off for a few more years a regime of Communism, and Reagan foreign policy advisors like United Nations ambassador Jeanne Kirkpatrick and Secretary of State Alexander Haig so frowned at the affinity that Latin American Christianity had for Marxist socialism that they found themselves telling journalists that four American churchwomen raped and slaughtered by the El Salvadoran National Guard on the highway to La Libertad were political activists who'd probably brought it on themselves—Secretary Haig even offered the ludicrous suggestion that the four churchwomen were first to engage the soldiers in gunfire.

López found no difficulty in choosing sides, aligning himself against the tyranny and terrorism of the former Nicaraguan regime and with the progressive, if imperfect, government of the Sandinistas. Word of his friendly relations with them got back to the Vatican Curia, however, and López was sent an official "visitor" from Rome who filed a confidential report, the upshot of which was that López was forced to give up his post as rector and went back to Spain for a sabbatical before heading to the University of Central America in San Salvador.

López's spirit seemed to have been broken for a time by his conflicts with the Catholic Church hierarchy, for though he was a forthright and sympathetic counselor to those who sought him out, he seemed hidden in the Jesuit residence, and his theology classes, though well prepared, were frankly thought to be dull. Yet in 1989 López found fresh vigor and happiness in his Sunday pastoral work in the farming region of Tierra Virgen, where his parishioners had such affection for him that twenty-five walked through San Salvador's killing zones in order to go to his funeral.

The oldest and most taciturn man in the Jesuit community was also the only native Salvadoran. José Joaquin López y López, who was called Lolo, was born in 1918 to a wealthy family that owned coffee plantations and a famous dairy in Santa Ana. Lolo felt called to the Catholic priesthood from his youth, finishing high school in a minor seminary before he was accepted into the Society of Jesus. While teaching upper-class boys at the *Externado San José*, he got the idea to hold weekend catechism classes for the poor, a ministry that finally became part of the Latin American organization *Fe y Alegría*, "Faith and Joy," and furnished El Salvador with thirteen schools and twelve workshops, as well as two health clinics with fifty thousand patients. Lolo financed it all in the old-fashioned way, with fund drives, government aid, and highly successful raffles.

Early in the 1960s López y López began campaigning for a Catholic university in San Salvador by going to right-wing politicians and the wealthiest families he knew with the hope of constructing a private alternative to the radicalized National University, so his humility and loyalty were put to the test when the focus on liberation theology offended the very groups he'd depended upon to found the UCA. Yet for many years he was general secretary to the faculty there and, at Ellacuría's behest, he joined the Jesuit community in 1988, knowing the threat of violence to them was persistent and gathering force, and knowing, too, he had prostate cancer and had few years more to live.

> "When the Son of man comes in his glory, and all the angels with him, then he will sit on his glorious throne. Before him will be gathered all the nations, and he will separate them one from another as a shepherd separates the sheep from the goats, and he will place the sheep at his right hand, but the goats at the left. Then the King will say to those at his right hand, 'Come, O blessed of my Father, inherit the kingdom prepared for you from the foundation of the world; for I was hungry and you gave me food, I was

> thirsty and you gave me drink, I was a stranger and you welcomed me, I was naked and you clothed me, I was sick and you visited me, I was in prison and you came to me.' Then the righteous will answer him, 'Lord, when did we see thee hungry and feed thee, or thirsty and give thee drink? And when did we see thee a stranger and welcome thee, or naked and clothe thee? And when did we see thee sick or in prison and visit thee?' And the King will answer them, 'Truly, I say to you, as you did it to one of the least of my brethren, you did it to me.'"
>
> (Mt 25:31–40)

By 1989, El Salvador's ten-year civil war had killed more than seventy thousand people and caused homelessness and misery for far more. Ellacuría had for a long time been urging dialogue between the factions and a negotiated settlement to end the war, and progress seemed slightly more possible when Alfredo Cristiani, the ARENA candidate, was elected president on March 19, and publicly committed his government to good-faith negotiations toward peace with the rebel forces of the *Frente Farabundo Martí de Liberación Nacional* (FMLN). But the Salvadoran government was arrogant, even belligerent, in its talks while—seemingly without Cristiani's awareness—the High Command heightened the violence against human rights organizations such as the National Trade Union Federation of Salvadoran Workers, the Committee of Mothers of the

Detained, Disappeared, and Assassinated, and even a primary school operated by the Lutheran Church. The FMLN halted negotiations and on November 11 initiated the largest offensive of the war, firing missiles at Cristiani's private home, the presidential residence, and the homes of the president and vice president of the Salvadoran Constituent Assembly.

Cristiani's response was to suspend all constitutional guarantees and announce a state of siege and a curfew between six at night and six in the morning. A huge counteroffensive of artillery and aerial bombardments of presumed guerilla hiding places in the poorest and most heavily populated areas of the city trapped families in their homes without food or water, or forced them to flee their neighborhoods and face gunfire in the streets. The government and armed forces seized the radio and television stations in order to have a national channel on which citizens could report guerilla activities and find lost members of their families, but the phone-in shows also became forums on which to broadcast attacks against what was thought to be the intellectual leadership behind the FMLN: Archbishop Rivera y Damas, the "Communists" infiltrating the Catholic Church, and, of course, the Jesuits. "Bring them to the public places and lynch them," one radio announcer insisted. Ellacuría, it was said, ought to be "spit to death."

President Cristiani was a graduate of Washington's Jesuit-run Georgetown University and was friendly with Ellacuría, but he was also thought to be in the thrall of the ultrarightist Roberto

D'Aubuisson, president of the assembly and founder of Cristiani's Nationalist Republican Alliance Party (ARENA), composed of paramilitary groups and wealthy industrial and farming interests. A "homicidal killer," as a former U. S. ambassador said of him, D'Aubuisson was said to be an admirer of the Nazis and their holocaust of the Jews, was rumored to have ordered the murder of Archbishop Oscar Romero, was the chief architect of the political assassinations, kidnappings, and terrorism of the underground death squads, and was officially ostracized by the United States in 1984 when it was found he'd tried to have Ambassador Thomas Pickering killed. Closely allied with D'Aubuisson was Colonel René Emilio Ponce, a shrewd tactician and former death squad member who was now Chief of the Joint General Staff and of a powerful corporate network of brutality and corruption that was financed by the United States.

On the afternoon of Monday, November 13, government officials established a zone of security around its Joint Command headquarters, the military academy, and the Arce neighborhood, which were in front of the main gate to the UCA. Three hundred soldiers were stationed around the campus, so presumably it was safe.

On Wednesday, November 15, an evening meeting of the High Command was held at the general staff headquarters, the *estado mayor.* Among the twenty-five present at the meeting were Colonel Ponce as well as Colonel Juan Orlando Zepeda, vice minister of defense, and Colonel Guillermo Benavides, director of the military academy. Worried about the offensive, the officers held hands and prayed for divine intervention, after which one of the commanders ordered the elimination of unionists and known members of the FMLN leadership. And Colonel Benavides, commanding officer of the security zone between the general staff headquarters and the UCA, was authorized to organize a commando unit within the Atlacatl Battalion for the purpose of assassinating Ellacuría and the other Jesuits. They were to leave no witnesses.

Ellacuría was in Spain at the first part of the offensive, visiting old friends and his ninety-three-year-old father, giving thanks for the five thousand dollar Alfonso Comín Prize awarded to the UCA for its commitment to justice for the oppressed, celebrating his fifty-ninth birthday, and being unanimously elected as president of the coordinating council of postgraduate institutions in Spain, Portugal, and Latin America, at which meeting he offered to host the council in his country in two years, "if I am still alive."

Ellacuría flew back to El Salvador on Monday, the thirteenth. With a curfew in effect and a state of siege having been declared, the twenty-three buildings on the shut-down university campus were bleakly empty but for the new Archbishop Romero Theological Reflection Center, a functional construction of concrete block that housed offices on the first floor and, on the second, the kitchen, dining room, guest room, and corridor of bedrooms of the Jesuit residence. Jon Sobrino had moved in before flying off to Thailand, but the six other priests were still shifting their hundreds of books and few other possessions from the old residence when Ellacuría got there.

A half hour later, as he was talking to his friends about Europe, they heard the doors to the Romero Center below them being kicked in. Hurrying downstairs the Jesuits found twenty soldiers from the elite Atlacatl Battalion rummaging through the offices. An officer who knew the Jesuits by their first names but who refused to identify himself told Ellacuría they were looking for hidden weapons and, given the state of siege, needed no permission to do so. After a thorough and orderly inspection of the upstairs residence, the two patrols left, searching no other buildings.

Ellacuría was fuming about it Tuesday morning when his Jesuit assistant, Rolando Alvarado, recalled his teens in Somoza's Nicaragua and told the rector that the intrusion was in fact a reconnaissance. Wouldn't it be wise for the Jesuits to go somewhere else?

Ellacuría replied that Alvarado was being paranoid, that the soldiers found nothing incriminating, and there were no other housing options anyway. "We have fought them from here and here we will stay."

His friend Ruben Zamora would later say, "Ignacio was a Cartesian, with absolute faith in logic. This time his analysis failed him."

Elba Ramos was the forty-two-year-old housekeeper at the Jesuit school of theology, a fifteen-minute walk away, and her husband, Obdulio, was a night watchman at the university when Father Amando López, who was in charge of buildings and grounds, gave the family of four the chance to live in a little guardhouse not far from the Jesuit residence. But the guardhouse was on Avenida Albert Einstein where the hammering noise of bombing was so frightening that Elba phoned the Jesuits to find out if there was a quieter place where she and her daughter Celina could stay for a while. Celina was sixteen and in the first year of a high school commercial course that was rigorous enough that she'd been forced to give up basketball and the band. She was having a hard time doing homework. On Sunday López offered Elba and Celina the guest room in the Archbishop Romero Theological Reflection Center where it was thought they'd have more peace and quiet.

Segundo Montes was installing telephones in the residence on Wednesday night, and Ignacio Martín-Baró took advantage of one in order to call his sister Alicia in Valladolid, Spain. He told her he was all right but that San Salvador was in a state of siege, and he held the telephone out so she could hear the bombs. "Oh, Nacho," she asked, "and when is this going to end?" "A lot more people will have to die yet," he told her. "A lot more people will have to die."

Lieutenant José Ricardo Espinoza was the twenty-eight-year-old commander of the commando unit within the feared Atlacatl Battalion and a graduate of the Special Warfare Center at Fort

Bragg, North Carolina. In fact, only the week before, thirteen Green Berets from the United States had flown in to oversee his company's training exercises. With the exercises called off because of the offensive, Espinoza's first assignment—an order hand-delivered by Colonel Ponce and signed by President Cristiani—had been the Monday night search of the Archbishop Romero Theological Reflection Center. A few of the Jesuits there he knew well, having been a high school student at the *Externado San José*. And so he was thought a natural for Wednesday night's assignment. Colonel Benavides had reportedly told him, "This is a situation where it's them or us; we are going to begin with the ringleaders. Within our sector we have the university and Ellacuría is there." Espinoza was told to use the tactic of Monday's search, but this time he was to eliminate Ellacuría. "And I want no witnesses," he said.

Espinoza objected that this was serious, but Colonel Benavides told him not to worry, that Espinoza had his support, meaning that of the High Command. On leaving, Espinoza asked the colonel's assistant, Lieutenant Yusshy Mendoza, for a bar of camouflage grease so that he could paint his face.

Espinoza's four patrols of thirty-six commandos assembled at the Captain General Gerardo Barrios Military Academy after midnight on Thursday, the sixteenth. With only two beige Ford 250 pickup trucks to get them to the university, five minutes away, there would have to be a return trip. The trucks took the Southern Highway then went uphill to the Mortgage Bank behind the UCA where the patrols finally were told who they'd be killing: priests who were in on the FMLN's offensive up to the hilt, furnishing logistical assistance to the guerillas and even overseeing their campaign against the armed forces and the people of El Salvador. Lieutenant Yusshy Mendoza, who was in charge of the operation, told Private Oscar Mariano Amaya, nicknamed Pilijay, or "Hangman" in the Nahuatl language, that it was he who would have prime responsibility for the assassinations because of his familiarity with the AK-47 rifle, a Soviet-made assault weapon wholly associated with the FMLN. When Pilijay was finished there would be a flare, at which time the four patrols would fire their rifles as if they were fighting off the fleeing terrorists.

Espinoza ordered them to form a column and head toward the university at about one A.M. on November 16, 1989. Electrical power was gone from the area but there was good light from the full moon. The pedestrian gate was forced open and the commandos hustled past the Chapel of Christ the Liberator to a parking lot where they feigned a first attack with the FMLN by riddling cars with bullets and throwing a grenade. A few soldiers must have then strayed off in the wrong direction, because a night watchman heard a voice say, "Don't go over there, there are only offices over there."

While some soldiers got on roofs of neighboring houses to watch, another group encircled the hillside and the Archbishop Romero Theological Reflection Center and began banging on the doors and windows, and a high fence of wire mesh was climbed so a first-floor door could be unlocked from the inside.

Sub-sergeant Tomás Zarpate went a few steps down a passageway when he heard a sound in a guest room and found Elba Ramos worriedly sitting on a divan bed beside a pretty teenaged girl who was lying under the covers. Lieutenant Yusshy Mendoza held a lamp up to see them and then told Zarpate to stay there and not let anyone leave. Ignacio Martín-Baró was being hauled down the passageway by a soldier when he saw Zarpate holding his rifle on the women. Eyewitness Lucía Barrera de Cerna heard Nacho say, "This is an injustice. You are carrion."

Pilijay saw a soldier forcing a piece of wood between a frame and a door when a priest in a coffee-colored robe frowned at them from his hammock on the balcony. Ellacuría said, "Wait. I am coming to open the door, but don't keep making so much noise." And then Pilijay heard his name being called and was told the priests were in the garden behind the residence.

Pilijay hurried out and found Sub-sergeant Antonio Ramiro Avalos, whose nickname was Satan, holding a rifle on five grim priests in pajamas or trousers and shirts, priests whom other Jesuits called *los viejos*, the old men, because their fifteen-hour days of hard work and anxiety had hurt their health and prematurely aged them. Ellacu, Nacho, Zeus, Pardito, Amando. Worried that it was five against two, Sub-sergeant Avalos ordered them to lie facedown on the grass, and then was called over by Lieutenant Espinoza, whose eyes were filling with tears because he saw that

Segundo Montes, his headmaster at the *Externado*, was among those on the ground. Espinoza impatiently asked, "When are you going to proceed?" Sergeant Avalos walked back to Pilijay and told him, "Let's proceed."

The five priests were prostrate just as they were in their rites of ordination when the litany of the saints was chanted. And they seemed to be whispering a psalmody when Sub-sergeant Avalos yelled, "Quick, quick, give it to them quickly!" and Pilijay fired the AK-47 at the heads of the three men in front of him, thinking their brains were the problem, killing Ignacio Ellacuría, Segundo Montes, and Ignacio Martín-Baró. Avalos fired his M16 at the heads and bodies of the two priests closest to him, Amando López and Juan Ramón Moreno, and then Pilijay finished off all five with a long burst from his fully automatic rifle. Only with difficulty would friends later be able to recognize the face of Amando López.

Sub-sergeant Zarpate heard the gunfire and then someone shouting, "Now!" Obediently he turned to Elba and Celina Ramos and, though they were far from being Communist agitators, Zarpate fired at them until "they no longer groaned," shooting Elba in the vagina in the signature style of the death squads. And then he glumly walked off.

In the first-floor Theological Reflection Center, offices were being trashed and commandos were firebombing the file cabinets, wiping out computers, burning books and tapes. When he heard the gun noise outside, one inflamed soldier looked up at a framed picture on the wall of a genial Archbishop Romero and fired a bullet at his heart.

A frail old man in a white undershirt walked out into the corridor and then to the front of the building. López y López was in hiding until he heard the gunfire, and then must have felt he had to go out. But when he saw his friends massacred on the grass, fear overtook him and he said, "Don't kill me, because I don't belong to any organization." And then he turned to go back inside the house.

Calling him "*Compa*," a nickname in the FMLN, the soldier ordered him him to come to him. Lolo walked on. But as he was entering a bedroom, he was hit with a shot and fell. Corporal Angel Pérez walked into the room to find what was in there. Like Sub-sergeant Avalos he was a graduate of a Small Unit Training Management Course in the United States. Lolo's hand took hold of his foot and in his astonishment Corporal Pérez fired twice at Joaquin López y López. And then, flushed with embarrassment at his surprise, he fired at the old man twice more.

Walking along a passageway toward the garden gate, Sub-sergeant Avalos heard groaning and lit a match to look into the guest room where Elba and Celina Ramos were still painfully alive and hugging each other in a widening pool of blood. The sergeant told Private Jorge Alberto Sierra to finish them off, and Sierra fired the full magazine of his M16 into them and trudged off, leaving bootprints of blood on the floor.

And then they were through. The whole operation had

taken no more than an hour. Pilijay headed back inside the Jesuit residence, wrecked the kitchen, and helped himself to a pilsner beer. Hoping to hide the fact that this was a formal execution, other commandos were ordered to haul the bodies back inside, but there was only time for Corporal Cotta Hernández to drag Juan Ramón Moreno along the tile floor to Jon Sobrino's bedroom, the red bundle of his brains hanging from his head. A book fell from its bookshelf there and into his flowing blood. The book's title was *The Crucified God.*

> **Behold, my servant shall prosper,**
> **he shall be exalted and lifted up, and shall be very high.**
> **As many were astonished at him . . .**
> **so shall he startle many nations;**
> **kings shall shut their mouths because of him;**
> **for that which has not been told them they shall see,**
> **and that which they have not heard they shall understand.**
>
> **(Is 52:13–15)**

The official story was that the murders were committed by the FMLN, and at first even Secretary of Defense Richard Cheney was firm in saying "there's no indication at all that the government of El Salvador had any involvement." Witnesses to the slayings were harassed and intimidated by the FBI; Colonel René Emilio Ponce, of all people, was put in charge of the official investigation of the murders; and the United States embassy all but stonewalled on the crimes. Word of the truth was getting out, however, and Massachusetts representative Joe Moakley's congressional task force finally embarrassed the Cristiani government into action, reflecting an old pattern in our relations with El Salvador over human rights issues in which, as Martha Doggett of the Lawyers Committee for Human Rights put it, "Washington plays the parent to the unruly Salvadoran child. When threats fail to curb behavior, punishment sometimes follows, though not as a rule." Eventually the Salvadoran Supreme Court charged four officers and five enlisted men with the crimes—a half measure certainly—and even though there were confessions from those who committed the atrocities, a jury that was possibly tampered with found only Colonel Guillermo Benavides and Lieutenant Yusshy Mendoza guilty of murder, the first officers ever convicted of a human rights violation. They would finally serve a little over a year of their thirty-year sentences. Each and every other member of the Atlacatl Battalion went free.

But the two-year investigation of the Jesuit murders shone a light on villains in the High Command, put an end to the hated security forces and the Atlacatl, focused attention on other crimes and inequities in El Salvador, and changed U. S. policy to one of full endorsement of negotiations, resulting in a peace agreement being signed in Chapultepec.

At the funeral of the six Jesuits, José María Tojeira, their provincial superior, offered a homily in which he ringingly said, "they have not killed the University of Central America and they have not killed the Society of Jesus in El Salvador." And the filled auditorium affirmed that with a two-minute standing ovation.

Two Salvadorans, two Americans, a Mexican, and a Canadian joined Jon Sobrino to again fill out the university's Jesuit community, and off the balcony where Ignacio Ellacuría frowned at the soldiers, a building extension was constructed to accomodate the growing numbers of theology students.

The blood of martyrs is the seed of the Church, wrote Tertullian. All the faithful do not perish, nor suffer infamy or risk, but Christians are expected to be witnesses to those who did, and do. And then we will find that like the martyrs before them, the two women and six Jesuits murdered in El Salvador are, as José María Tojeira has written, dead "who continue to be profoundly active and alive . . . generating human spirit, generating human dignity, generating the capacity for dialogue and humane rationality, generating a critical capacity, a constructive capacity, and generating imagination."

Eucharist

"At the request of some friends and many parishioners," the Right Reverend Patrick Aloysius Flanagan wrote in 1956, he "'weakened' to the point of consenting to put, in pamphlet form," eight articles he'd written on the sacrament of the Eucharist. Culled from three hundred of his so-called "effusions" on religious topics in the Sunday bulletins that were handed out in the vestibule, It Is the Mass That Matters *was his Christmas gift to the congregation of Holy Angels Church.*

I was just nine then, and the sentences were too hard for me, as they may have been to the majority of those in the pews. With only a handful of college graduates among the five hundred families, ours was a working-class parish, and I wonder how many finished or fully understood his twenty-seven-page meditation, or even appreciated the wit and dexterity of his nineteenth-century prose:

"If I had the wildest suspicion of publishing [these pieces] in this printed form," he wrote in his explanatory foreword, "I would, no doubt, have given more care to the language and construction. To attempt such

'decoration' now would not be the 'labor of love' of their original composition—but one of disagreeable work and not a little industry. Apart from this latter consideration I don't think it would be smart to noticeably change their original 'dress,' lest I might be suspected of using a ghost writer."

His first chapter title was "A Few Infinitely Important Convictions For Every Adult Catholic Regarding The Sacrifice Of The Mass." And that was followed by "Some Further, More Than Thrilling, Thoughts About The Mass, Entirely Distinct From An Attempted Doctrinal Discussion." Monsignor's seventh chapter was headed, "Are Some Readers Of The Recent Bulletins Still Lacking The Mentally-Satisfying Convictions Of The 'Purpose' And The 'Place' Of The Mass In Any Worthwhile Service Of The Blessed Trinity?"

In the company of women, Monsignor was dashing, funny, impatient, and powerfully masculine, with milk-white hair and rimless glasses and just a wink of the sly old rogue in him, the Irish grand lion amidst his pride of dutiful daughters. My father, who was as much a general as he was an engineer, a man not easily intimidated, who did not readily smile, used to cringe and grin in the old priest's presence, just as all the others in the Men's Club and Knights of Columbus did. We children generally missed the self-effacing humor and irony in Monsignor's tyrannical ways. Somehow the zeal in his terrorism told adults he was kidding; we were too naive and genuine to get it. And so we could be paralyzed with fear whenever he chose to give us religious instruction.

Monsignor Flanagan would simply barge into a classroom, surprising the teacher, and at once whatever subject we'd been on would be forgotten. "Why did God make us?" Monsignor would ask, and thirty hands would shoot up. We wanted to catch that easy one from the first pages of The Baltimore Catechism, *for if a child answered with sufficient ignorance, Monsignor might thunder, "Sit down, you buzzard!" or "Go back to kindergarten, you double-barreled boob!" And soon, we knew, he'd be on to harder quizzing, scowlingly asking questions the great theologians pondered, questions we couldn't be expected to understand fully. What is meant by sanctifying grace? What is the difference between a mortal and venial sin? Why did Christ have to die to redeem us? Once in a while I could see the sisters who taught us get a look of mystery and terror on their own faces as they, too, tried to figure out the correct response. At other times I'd notice a sister stifling laughter at a joke that was way over our heads, and I'd wonder how she could chuckle like that when he was so serious.*

Within the hour he was through with us, and he signaled it by letting a child's wrong answer stagger him. Seemingly faint, Monsignor tilted into the teacher's desk to take the heavy weight from his legs. "Children," he said, "I can't go on." And he sighed with great disappointment as he said, "It's my heart. My heart is . . . black. As black as this cassock." Waving a frail, dying man's goodbye, he asked, "Won't somebody help me out? I can't do it on my own. Hansen!"

I shot up, alert.

"Come up here and help me out."

Worriedly, I walked forward, and he leaned some of his great size onto me.

"And the rest of you," he weakly said, "go back to your books and try to get an education. I see I have failed . . . utterly."

With confusion and not a little fear, I enabled him to the door and the hallway, and there he smiled and left me to go with zest to other rooms.

Even now I stand in that hallway, watching his white Roman collar and striding cassock as the old priest recedes into the past. Catholicism has changed a great deal since then, and authoritarian semigods like him are as gone as the kings of Persia. But I feel graced for having been taught by him, and to imitate in my own life his unsentimental reverence for Christ in the Eucharist.

EUCHARIST

I first received Christ in the Eucharist in 1955. It was December 8, the feast of Mary's Immaculate Conception, and my brother Rob and I were celebrating our eighth birthday. And because of that, or because we were such gosh darn cute twins, we were given the honor of leading the sixty-child procession of second graders to the altar rail of Holy Angels Church, in Omaha. We wore new shoes, navy blue slacks, white shirts with red cufflinks, and white clip-on ties. We'd slicked down our hair with Wildroot Creme Oil. We felt spiffy.

I have no recollection of the Mass or of the homily preached by Monsignor Patrick Aloysius Flanagan, the younger brother of Boys Town's founder. But my memory is helped by Kodachrome snapshots that were taken of our procession toward the high altar, our hands folded and fingers steepled, our faces solemn, reverent, and way on the other side of cool and insouciant. We'd been catechized to feel awe for the mystery of Christ's presence in the sacrament we'd receive, but we'd heard from older kids on the playground that the Host tasted horrible and Rob was afraid he'd hate it and yet be punished with hellfire if he spit it out. And I was full of childish wonder about the changes Jesus would make in me. Would I be a Superman, a holy man, a healer? Would homework now be easier? Would I be a wiz? Or would I be jailed in piety, condemned to sinlessness, obedience, and no fun?

We knelt at a polished marble altar railing and, lest the Blessed Sacrament fall onto our unconsecrated hands, hid them under the drapery of a railing-long linen cloth. I peeked at Monsignor Flanagan sidling along, holding up the Host to my classmates as he recited Latin and laid the thin round wafer on their tongues.

Then Monsignor was in front of me in his gold-embroidered white vestments, a seemingly towering figure, as stern and intimidating as the destroying God of Abraham. I felt the cold touch of the paten against my throat as a cynical eighth grade altar boy in black cassock and white surplice held it under my chin, and with humility and childish worry I stuck out my drying tongue like a toddler being fed from a spoon. Watching the Host, I heard Monsignor say as he made the sign of the cross with it, "*Corpus Dómini nostri Jesu Christi custódiat ánimam tuam in vitam aetérnam. Amen.*" May the Body of our Lord Jesus Christ preserve your soul into life everlasting. So be it. And in spite of my unworthiness, he gave me First Communion.

I hesitated, then stood, huddling a little as I walked back to my pew under the smiles of my father and mother and the ever-wary gaze of Sister Mary Evans, my second grade teacher—still feeling the wafer like plastic on the roof of my mouth, but not disliking the taste. Then I knelt heedfully upright and mentally prayed as we'd been instructed to do, some scared and scientific part of me assaying myself for chemical reactions or a sudden infusion of wisdom while fancying Christ now sitting dismally in my scoundrel soul, my oh so many sins pooling like sewer water at his sandaled feet. But soon I saw that I was still me; there would be no howls of objection, no immediate correction or condemnation, no hint that I was under new management, just the calming sense that whoever I was was fine with Jesus.

It was a grace I hadn't imagined.

The first Jewish followers of the Way of Jesus of Nazareth primarily evangelized other Jews like themselves, just as their Messiah had, but soon took the good news of the life and teachings of Jesus to Gentiles, and for those non-Jews translated *b'rakhah,* the Hebrew word for "blessing," with the Greek word *eucharistia*, or "thanksgiving." And so, though the word *Eucharist* is never used in the New Testament, it became by association the common name for what Catholics call the Mass.

The first writing of any sort to mention Christ's Last Supper is Paul's first letter to the Corinthians, sent in the year 54:

> For I received from the Lord what I also handed on to you, that the Lord Jesus on the night when he was betrayed took a loaf of bread, and when he had given thanks, he broke it and said, "This is my body that is for you. Do this in remembrance of me." In the same way he took the cup also, after supper, saying, "This cup is the new covenant in my blood. Do this, as often as you drink it, in remembrance of me." For as often as you eat this bread and drink the cup, you proclaim the Lord's death until he comes. (1 Cor 11:23–26)

Twenty to thirty years later, the evangelists Mark, Matthew, and Luke developed their own, non-eyewitness accounts of Christ's last Passover meal in their Gospels, interpreting an inherited Aramaic tradition that the first generation of Christians thought was faithful to what Jesus actually said and did on that Thursday night.

In the liturgical practice of the Catholic Church the first three gospel accounts have been conflated into one text:

> *The day before he suffered*
> *he took bread into his sacred hands*
> *and looking up to heaven,*
> *to you, his almighty Father,*
> *he gave you thanks and praise.*
> *He broke the bread,*
> *gave it to his disciples, and said:*
> *Take this, all of you, and eat it:*
> *this is my body which will be given up for you.*

When supper was ended,
he took the cup.
Again he gave you thanks and praise,
gave the cup to his disciples, and said:
Take this, all of you, and drink from it:
this is the cup of my blood,
the blood of the new and everlasting covenant.
It will be shed for you and for all
so that sins may be forgiven.
Do this in memory of me.

Everlasting covenant. Religious Jews had, and have, far stronger associations with the word covenant than most Christians do, for it was their forefathers' hard-won covenant with God that formed them into a nation, and fidelity to that covenant was the overriding concern of their religious, social, and national existence.

In biblical times to remember meant not only to recall to mind whatever had been done by God but also to effectively experience it again, to have the past authentically present. Remembering, the Jews would be conscious of God's intervention in their history and, in gratitude for that, be called to holy action now.

And so it was with the apostles. Hearing Christ's words at the Last Supper, they would have harkened back to the Exodus when Moses mediated the covenant between God and the

Israelite tribes, forming them into one people, concluding and sealing the promise with the blood of slaughtered animals, and celebrating its enactment with a feast. (Ex 24:4–11.) Only after Christ's crucifixion and resurrection, however, would the apostles have seen that Christ had offered *himself* as a sacrifice and mediated a *new* covenant of salvation for them. The letter to the Hebrews puts it this way: "But when Christ came as a high priest . . . he entered once for all into the Holy Place, not with the blood of goats and calves, but with his own blood, thus obtaining eternal redemption." (Heb 9:11–12.)

With the feast of Passover (otherwise known as the feast of *matzah*, unleavened bread) the Jews commemorated God's great act of salvation in "passing over" their own homes—so signified with the blood of a lamb—as the firstborn sons of the Egyptians were slain. They commemorated, too, the flight of the Israelites from Egypt after four hundred years of slavery; their passage through the Sea of Reeds; the sealing of the covenant at Sinai; and their final conquest of Canaan, the foretold land of milk and honey.

In the time of Christ, the feast could only be celebrated in Jerusalem. Just before sundown on the fourteenth day of Nisan, the first month of the year, lambs were slaughtered in the Temple by the heads of households, and high priests poured out the collected blood at the foot of the altar of sacrifice. Jesus, as the highest-ranking member of a *chaburah*, or brotherhood, would have fulfilled the functions of the head of household and ritually killed and roasted the lamb, then carried it to a festive and illuminated guest room, *kataluma* in Greek—the same word that is generally translated as "inn" in the narrative of Christ's birth. The Jerusalem *kataluma* was, according to the gospel of Luke, furnished with soft, pillowed couches horseshoed around a low table so that the guests could recline on the brace of their left elbows and have their right hands free for eating. The format was not only that of a Seder and a hospitality meal welcoming those on a journey, but also that of a Hellenistic symposium, or a convivial intellectual conversation nurtured by wine. According to the gospel of John, in this meal the focus of conversation was a farewell discourse by Jesus.

We know from his criticism of Simon the Pharisee (Lk 7:44–46.) that Jesus valued the Jewish customs associated with the gracious hosting of a meal, so we can presume that in his role as host of the feast of *Pesach* (*Pascha* in Greek), Jesus would have kissed his guests in greeting them, anointed their heads with perfumed oil, and as we see in the gospel of John, washed their feet, just as slaves did then. Commencing the feast, Jesus would have first offered a prayer of thanksgiving to bless the fruit of the vine and then passed the cup, or chalice, of wine to his friends to share. Then the flat cakes of unleavened *matzah*—the so-called bread of affliction—would have been served along with a kind of leek, *maror*, that was dipped in a dish of salted water and vinegar. After that the lamb would have been brought to the table.

To the question "Why is this night different from all other

nights?" Jesus would have recited the *Haggadah*, or narrative of the memorial rite, recalling the events of the Exodus: "We were slaves of Pharaoh in Egypt and the Eternal, our God, brought us out from there with a strong hand and an outstretched arm. Now if God had not brought out our forefathers from Egypt, then even we, our children, and our children's children might still have been enslaved to Pharaoh in Egypt."

With the pouring of a second cup of wine, Jesus would have continued the remembrance—in liturgical terms, the *anamnesis*—concluding it with praise of the Eternal God in what Jews call the Great Hallel: Psalms 114 and 115:1–8. All who were there would have then shared the wine and finished eating the *matzah* and lamb and, perhaps, stewed fruit. Jesus would have blessed a third cup of wine with the second half of the Hallel, singing a hymn made up of Psalms 115:9–18, 116, and 117. The feast would have ended just around midnight. And then, the Gospels tell us, Jesus and his disciples went to a garden across the Kidron Valley from Jerusalem, on the hill of the Mount of Olives, in order to continue their prayer.

With about fifteen other classmates, Rob and I became altar boys in sixth grade. There were no altar girls then, and we were not acolytes, as in other religious denominations, for in Roman Catholicism with its hints, always, of incense and cowls and medieval cathedrals, the acolyte designation formally belongs just below that of deacon and is the highest ranking of the four minor orders, above exorcist, lector, and ostiary (or door-keeper).

To become an altar boy, we'd had to pass an oral exam on the pronunciation and memorization of the Latin of the Tridentine Rite in a four-page booklet of Mass responses, and a walk-through exam on our suave reverence in serving the priest: genuflecting to Christ in the tabernacle without tilting or grunting, shifting the Roman Missal from the epistle side to the gospel side of the altar with such effortless silence that the book seemed to have been spirited there, trickling wine into the chalice at the Offertory with all the seriousness of a sommelier at a four-star restaurant, ringing the handbells at the Consecration for just the length of a Jesus, Mary, and Joseph.

At that jaunty and guileless age I had no inkling of the queasy stage fright I'd feel at my first weekday 6:30 A.M. Mass when I walked out to the high altar in my cassock and surplice with an older altar boy and the holy terror of Monsignor Flanagan, nor of the seeming thirty-minute agony of reciting in halting and arduous Latin my first "*Confiteor,*" nor of the fear and panic that would roost in my chest as I failed to predict one after another of the Monsignor's extremely particular expectations.

At the "*Hanc igitur,*" when it was time for the Consecration, we two servers humbly ascended the three plush, carpeted steps of the high altar to kneel beside Monsignor Flanagan, the older boy on the right side handling the ringing of four joined bells. The red-lettered rubrics of the Sacramentary called for the priest to pronounce the words of Consecration, genuflect, adore the Host for a moment, rise, elevate the Host for all the congregation behind him to see, replace it on the paten, and genuflect once again. We held the hem of his knee-length chasuble so Monsignor could do all that without interference. I was wholly focused on doing it right, and grateful that I wasn't also in charge of ringing the bells, when the old white-haired priest hunched forward and, holding the Host in his index fingers and thumbs, slowly, softly, and reverently recited the Latin translation of Christ's words at the Last Supper, "*Hoc est enim Corpus meum.*" For this is my Body. And a little later, Monsignor hunched over the tilted chalice, speaking into it as he slowly and scrupulously recited, "*Hic est enim Calix Sánguinis mei, novi et ætérni testaménti: mystérium fídei: qui pro vobis et pro multis effundítur in remissiónem peccatórum.*" For this is the Chalice of my Blood of the new and eternal covenant: the mystery of faith: which shall be shed for you and for many unto the forgiveness of sins. "*Hæc quotiescúmque fecéritis, in mei memóriam faciétis.*" As often as you shall do these things, in memory of me shall you do them.

I was in awe. My theology of the Real Presence was that of a sixth grader, and my Latin was in its infancy, so large parts of the history and lore of the sacrament were going way over my head, but I felt privileged to be there and observe from up close the mystery in which Christ's body and blood were somehow actually confected from ordinary bread and wine. If my own faith had not confirmed the fact of that event, Monsignor

Flanagan's faith in it surely would have. *All you have heard*, he seemed to be saying, *is true.*

And when on other days I would glimpse Monsignor in the priest's sacristy before Mass, kneeling with arthritic pain on his prie-dieu, and solemnly adoring Christ in the tabernacle, I would understand that if it *was* all true, if Jesus was really there, you'd be insolent and vain to do other than what the old priest so reverently did.

In Luke's gospel, the life of Jesus is full of journeys in which he is dependent on the hospitality of friends and strangers for his food and lodging. Even at his birth, Jesus was laid in a manger—the trough in a barn from which cattle feed—because there was no room for the holy family in an inn. Thirty years later, during his public ministry, as Jesus and his disciples were walking toward a village, Luke writes that a voice cried out, "'I will follow you wherever you go.' And Jesus said to him, 'Foxes have holes, and birds of the air have nests; but the Son of Man has nowhere to lay his head.'" (Lk 9:57–58.) Jesus was frankly and unashamedly dependent on the graciousness of others, and fulfilled to perfection the highly choreographed customs of ancient hospitality by which a stranger gradually becomes a guest.

Ten meals are featured in Luke's gospel. There is the banquet at the house of Levi, where Pharisees complain that Jesus is eating and drinking with tax collectors and sinners, and he answers, "'I have come to call not the righteous but sinners to repentance.'" (Lk 5:32.) There is a dinner with the Pharisee named

Simon, at which a notorious woman weeps at the feet of Jesus, dries his feet with her hair, finds reconciliation, and inspires the parable of the forgiving creditor who was loved most by the one whose debt was largest.

In the third meal, at "a deserted place" in Bethsaida, Luke hints at associations with the Sinai experience of Israel's flight from Egypt as he tells how Jesus miraculously fed five thousand using a eucharistic formula that in Luke's time would have been familiar to all Christians: "And taking the five loaves and two fish, he looked up to heaven, and blessed and broke them, and gave them to the disciples to set before the crowd. And all ate and were filled." (Lk 9:16–17.)

On a journey to Jerusalem, Jesus is apparently alone when he visits the home of an unmarried woman named Martha—a scandalous act in those times. There Martha's sister Mary sits at his feet as if she were his student, an impudence for females then, as is seen when Martha insists Jesus tell her sister to help with the serving, *diakonia*—the term Luke will use for ministry to the community in Acts. Jesus immediately assesses the actual cause of Martha's anxiety; it is not that she is taxed with many household chores but that she's neglected the one thing that would give meaning to her service, which is being in his presence and hearing his wisdom.

In the next chapter, Jesus is invited to a noon meal at the home of a Pharisee whose strict interpretation of Jewish law incites him to shame Jesus for failing to carry out the formalities of hand-washing and purification of cup and dish before he sat to eat. Jesus responds by indicting as hypocrites those Pharisees and scholars of the law who concentrate on the ostentations of religion while simultaneously ignoring religion's call to justice for others and a full and abiding love of God.

The host at his next meal is a Pharisee of greater importance, the featured guests are scribes and lawyers, and the dinner, which seems to be a formal Hellenistic symposium, is being held on the Sabbath. All there watch Jesus closely and are offended when on a holy day Jesus heals a man with dropsy, an effusion of fluid into the skin and muscle tissues that causes painful swelling. Jesus counters their feelings of insult with parables that focus on the shared meal as a fulfillment of the purpose of the Sabbath—that is, to nourish health and hope and solidarity with the poor, the lame, the blind, the oppressed, and all who hear the word of God and act on it.

Concern for justice and the poor is also highlighted in the story of hospitality in the house of Zacchaeus, the chief tax collector in Jericho and a wealthy man short in stature. Wanting to see the famous prophet he thinks of as Lord, but held far off by the crowds, Zacchaeus scrabbles up a sycamore tree, but is soon called down by Jesus, who says it is necessary for him to be Zacchaeus's houseguest, meaning that in his stay with Zacchaeus Jesus will fulfill his mission of offering salvation to sinners, "'for the Son of Man has come to seek and save what was lost.'" (Lk 19:10.)

Reading over these stories I have been struck by how wanting in fun and food and relaxation these dinners seemed to be. Jesus is constantly quizzed or critiqued or compelled to act as a mediator in our gospel accounts, but there must have been hundreds of meals with friends and hospitable strangers during his three-year public ministry, dinners filled with graciousness, good food and wine, and maybe even hilarity. There are jests and puns and comic situations throughout the New Testament—Christ's dealings with his enemies are never without irony or wordplay—but there is also a grimness in the evangelists that probably has its origins in the persecutions that the first-century Christians were undergoing.

And so it is sometimes necessary for me to remember noontime dinners on Sundays. Eight A.M. Mass would be just a memory and the Omaha *World-Herald* would be scattered about the living room as we sat down to my mother's pot roast, boiled potatoes, and canned vegetables, with canned fruit cocktail for dessert. Dad would retell comic incidents from his job as an electrical engineer for the Omaha Public Power District. My three older sisters or Rob would talk about what our teachers said at school, or what chums did to annoy them, or what their schemes were for the afternoon. Mom would talk about the content of phone calls or letters she'd gotten from old friends or relatives. Reaching for a second helping, I'd probably spill my glass of milk. And in that serene, good-natured, *Ozzie and Harriet* setting we each got a sense of where we'd been, who we were, and what we hoped to become. It gave us our identity, not just as a family of two parents and five children, but as unique individuals within that grouping.

Jesus was doing that in all his meals, singling out his hosts and guests as highly individual children of God, admonishing, praising, or helping them as they needed, and yet generalizing in ways that are instructive to us even today. And that is never more true than in his ascent to Jerusalem where the fundamental themes of the seven previous meals are remembered and combined in the stunning climax of his Last Supper. There a new Paschal mystery is introduced, that of Christ "passing over" to his Father and redeeming creation through his life, death, resurrection, ascension, and exaltation. As presented in Luke, the supper is a liturgical event in which Christ offers thanksgiving to God and shares the *matzah* with his friends, connecting those actions—through the metonymy "body"—with the affliction he will suffer on the Cross. In like manner Christ offers thanksgiving and shares the cup of wine, connecting those actions with the blood he will shed and the blood of the new covenant foretold more than six hundred years earlier by the prophet Jeremiah:

> The days are surely coming, says the LORD, when I will make a new covenant with the house of Israel and the house of Judah. . . . I will put my law within them, and I will write it on their hearts; and I will be their God, and they shall be my people. No longer shall they teach one another, or say to each other, "Know the LORD," for they shall all know me,

from the least of them to the greatest, says the LORD; for I will forgive their iniquity, and remember their sin no more.

(Jer 31:31–34.)

The first seven meals featured Jesus as prophet. At the Last Supper, Jesus asserted by word and symbol that he was the *Mashiach*, the Christ, and commanded his apostles to share similar meals in memorial of his life, passion, and resurrection, in such a way making Christ truly present again as sacrifice, redeemer, and Lord. Celebrated worthily, with faith in the power of the Holy Spirit, that memorial would be a sacrament in which Christ himself would be at work, healing and transforming others and uniting them to himself.

There would be two other, postresurrection meals in Luke, the first of them in Emmaus, seven miles from Jerusalem, with a disciple named Cleopas and another unnamed disciple, possibly his wife. Each was probably to become an elder, *presbyteros*, in the early Church. Confused by reports of the resurrection, Cleopas and the other disciple were heatedly discussing the amazing things that had gone on since the feast of *Pesach*, when they were joined on the road by a sojourner to Jerusalem. He at first seemed in the dark about the crucifixion of Jesus and the shock of his rising from the dead, but then the stranger called them foolish for their failure to understand the significance of the Passion, and interpreted the Torah and all the prophets for them as a way of explaining why Jesus had to die. Their hearts on fire due to his inspiring teaching, they invited the man to stay with them in Emmaus and there, offering the *b'rakhah*, he broke the *matzah* and handed it to them, and they finally realized their guest was Jesus himself. And then he became invisible to them.

In their excitement Cleopas and the other disciple hurried back to Jerusalem to inform the huddled Eleven of what Jesus had said and done, and the risen Jesus appeared there as well, calming those who were frightened that he was a ghost by showing them his injured hands and feet. "While in their joy they were disbelieving and wondering, he said to them, 'Have you anything to eat?' They gave him a piece of broiled fish, and he took it and ate in their presence." (Lk 24:41–43.) That was the tenth and final meal, for afterward Jesus blessed them and ascended to heaven.

The Jesus who was symbolic food at his birth, lying with straw in a manger, or cattle trough, is later seen sharing food with others throughout his public ministry, becomes real food and wine at his Last Supper, and in his final meeting with his apostles was teaching them to feed and serve others. And in blessing them he was fulfilling God's two-thousand-year-old promise to Abraham, that in his offspring all the families on earth would be blessed.

Were I asked for a shorthand version of what the Mass is, I need do no more than quote the lyrics of a song by Marty Haugen: "We remember how you loved us to your death, and still we celebrate for you are with us here. And we believe that we will see you when you come in your glory, Lord. We remember, we celebrate, we believe."

The first Jewish converts to the Way of Christ did that as well, for in Luke's Acts of the Apostles we find: "They devoted themselves to the apostles' teaching and fellowship, to the breaking of bread and the prayers. . . . Day by day, as they spent much time together in the temple, they broke bread at home and ate their food with glad and generous hearts, praising God and having the goodwill of all the people." (Acts 2:42–47.)

In the instructions on "the way of life" in the *Didache* of the late first century, a strong Judaic heritage can be seen in the blessings of the first eucharistic celebrations:

> Now about the Eucharist: This is how to give thanks. First in connection with the cup:
>
> We thank you, our Father, for the holy vine of David, your child, which you have revealed through Jesus, your child [servant]. To you be glory forever.
>
> Then in connection with the broken bread:
>
> We thank you, our Father, for life and knowledge which you have revealed through Jesus, your child. To you be glory forever.

Writing to Emperor Antoninus Pius in 155, Justin Martyr tried to explain Christian practices, giving us a fascinating portrait of how liturgical—and familiar— their celebrations had become in just fifty years.

> On the day we call the day of the sun, all who dwell in the city or country gather in the same place. The memoirs of the apostles and the writings of the prophets are read, as much as time permits. When the reader has finished, he who presides over those gathered admonishes and challenges them to imitate these beautiful things. Then we all rise together and offer prayers for ourselves . . . and for all others, wherever they may be, so that we may be found righteous by our life and actions, and faithful to the commandments, so as to obtain eternal salvation. When the prayers are concluded we exchange the kiss. Then someone brings bread and a cup of water and wine mixed together to him who presides over the brethren. He takes them and offers praise and glory to the Father of the universe, through the name of the Son and of the Holy Spirit and for a considerable time he gives thanks that we have been judged worthy of these gifts. When he has concluded the prayers and thanksgiving, all present give voice to an acclamation by saying: "Amen." When he who presides has given thanks and the people have responded, those whom we call deacons give to those present the "eucharisted" bread, wine and water and take them to those who are absent.

Christ's encounter with Cleopas and the unnamed disciple on the journey to Emmaus—interpreting Scripture for them and blessing, breaking, and sharing the bread—had provided second-century Christians with the structure for a eucharistic ritual that is still fundamentally the same after nearly two thousand years.

We still assemble on Sundays in a church or home for a gathering at which Christ himself presides in the person of a bishop or priest. Introductory prayers and a penitential rite collect us as one, acquaint us with the season or feast, and prepare us for the Liturgy of the Word. In Christ's time a service in the synagogue called for two readings from the scrolls and the singing of a psalm, and so it is that we read an extract from the Hebrew scriptures and from the epistles, and a psalm and Alleluia are sung, and then we hear a gospel account of the life of Jesus, the fulfillment of God's word. A homily or instruction is followed by a confession of faith, usually the Nicene Creed, and a series of intercessory prayers of Jewish origin, for the needs of the Church, the nation, the locality, the persecuted, the sick, or those who have died.

The Liturgy of the Eucharist recalls the four verbs of the institution narratives: Jesus took, blessed, broke, gave. In this, the former Canon of the Mass, we begin with what used to be called the Offertory, in which Christians unite their own lives with Christ's life and ministry in the self-offering of their words and deeds in the gifts of bread and wine. Receiving the gifts, the priest articulates the faith and action of the congregation in offering thanksgiving to God with a variation on the *Kiddush*, a Jewish blessing, and after some preparatory rites commences the great eucharistic prayer by which the Church is created, enacted, and characterized. The prayer is introduced by one of ninety-one prefaces for various liturgical seasons and feasts, which is concluded with the *Sanctus*, the "Holy, holy, holy" that greeted Jesus on his final entrance to Jerusalem. The preface is followed by the *epiclesis*, or solemn invocation of the Holy Spirit on the gifts; the Consecration, or narrative of Christ's institution of this memorial at the Last Supper; and the *anamnesis*, or the act of remembrance that makes Christ's actions present and invites the faithful to recall their own crucifixions and resurrections. In communion with the worldwide Church, we then join in a memorial prayer, interceding for all Christians living and dead, that they may find light, happiness, and peace in the presence of God, through Christ "from whom all good things come."

The Doxology, a hymn of praise to the Holy Trinity, concludes the great eucharistic prayer and leads into the Communion Rite where the faithful first recite "The Lord's Prayer," recalling that we are one family with God as our Father, and then we offer each other a handshake, hug, or kiss as a sign of peace, unity, intimacy, and love. Tertullian called it "the seal of prayer." The Host or bread is broken in the "fraction rite" and shared, as at a family meal, when the congregation goes forward to the banquet table, as on their journey to the heavenly kingdom, and receive in faith the body and blood of Christ.

Catholic theology teaches that sacraments effect what they signify, and so it is here. Our gifts of bread and wine are changed by Christ from being symbols of ourselves and our self-giving, to being Christ himself and his self-giving. They are no longer things; they are God. And in this extravagant gift of the Eucharist we are, as Saint Augustine wrote, receiving ourselves, for our Baptism formed us into the body of Christ and his members. Our "Amen," our "So be it," is a sign that we are both receiving and giving, that Christ has not just become present to us, but that we have become present to Christ. The liturgical celebration is concluded after silent prayer of adoration, gratitude, and petition, and we are sent out as Christ's disciples to love and serve God and one another, with a blessing in the name of the Father, and of the Son, and of the Holy Spirit.

With Constantine the Great's miraculous conversion to Christianity in the year 312, he altered, for good and ill, the nature of the Church of Rome. Rather than being a contrarian, Mediterranean religion, it became worldwide and, at its worst, imperialist. Rather than being persecuted, it was now legally sanctioned, privileged, increasingly wealthy, but shackled by its too cozy alliance with the interests and intrigues of monarchies. And churches themselves took on that royal character, becoming grand as palaces, as opulent as theaters, with magnificent paintings and ornate altars positioned like high thrones, and with rood screens and communion railings to hold the laity at bay. Christ's instruction to Mary Magdalene just after his resurrection, *Nolo me tangere*, "Don't touch me," was used continually as a theme in art to school the masses in a needed separation between the ordained and the not. The Liturgy of the Eucharist was no longer an action of the assembly but the sole and private action of a priest whose back was to them so he could face Christ the King in the tabernacle and concentrate on confecting the sacrament in whispered secrecy. To the illiterate and generally uncatechized masses, it was no less than magic and sorcery; and they watched with a mixture of gratitude and wonder as the priest interceded for them and inveigled a seemingly judgmental and damning God out of heaven and into their midst with the Latin words of consecration they misheard as "hocus-pocus." Reception of Communion by the laity became so rare and their theology so childish that it was possible to bruit about the old wives' tale that the Host would bleed if scratched.

The Reformation was a protest against such a Church, one that in a millennium of chaotic growth and political chicanery had become shoddy, disorderly, disreputable, and adrift from its biblical roots. Countering and condemning that Reformation, the Council of Trent—which met intermittently in Trento, Italy, between 1545 and 1563—actually did much to address the grievances that made Protestantism inevitable and the council necessary. It disciplined the financial dealings of the Roman Curia, inaugurated rigorous standards for priestly formation in seminaries, determined the meaning and number of the sacraments, and with the call for the publication of a *Missal Romanum*, homogenized the liturgy of the Mass, which had theretofore as many variations in the West as there were countries where it was celebrated.

Clarifying its position in contradistinction to many Protestant sects, the Council of Trent also declared that Christ sacrifices himself in the Mass just as he did on the Cross, and through Christ, our immolated victim and priest, the Mass itself becomes an unbloody sacrifice of praise, thanksgiving, and commemoration, through which the merits of Christ's redeeming death are applied to the souls of the living and the dead for the expiation of sin. And Trent made it official Catholic teaching that in the consecrated elements of bread and wine, Christ is not just a spiritual presence, but a real one; that in the Eucharist the elements were transubstantiated into Christ's body and blood to such a degree that nothing of the bread and wine remained beyond what metaphysicians call accidentals.

The city of Trento was called Tridentum in ancient times, so the Latin liturgy of its *Roman Missal* came to be called the Tridentine Mass. Erring on the side of inclusion, embellishment, redundancy, and piety, the Missal prescribed as necessities those ancillary prayers, such as the prologue to John's gospel, that may have been part of the private devotions of ministers in some countries. Even when a choir chanted a text, the priest was required to secretly recite it, as if the song of the unordained would not be heard by God. But there was a dignity, grandness, and pageantry to the ceremonies it made obligatory. The goal seemed to have been to inspire awe and reverence and a sense of holy mystery in the laity, and that it managed to do.

My family were happy parishioners in an old, American-Irish Catholicism, when the church and school and social hall of Holy Angels filled our days with lessons, novenas, rosaries, meetings, choir practice, the major sports, pancake breakfasts, spaghetti dinners, bake sales, dances, and other activities, and it was not unusual to get there for Mass before eight in the morning and leave after eight at night.

We were ever aware, though, that it was the Mass that was central. An old visiting priest once harangued us schoolchildren in his homily, "If you truly believed what is going on here," and he gestured toward the high altar and tabernacle, "you'd be here every day!" And we looked to each other in puzzlement: we *were* there every day; it was the first thing we did before going to the classrooms for religion and the five other, lesser subjects.

The holy nuns who were our teachers taught us to see the Mass as the occasion where the hunger of our heart would find satisfaction. In fact, it came to seem there was a hole in the day when, on vacation or for some other reason, we did not go to church. I feel that way still.

Jesus taught his disciples to pray, "Give us this day our daily bread," and as the concept of the eucharistic mystery developed over the centuries, the frequency of its celebration increased from weekly assemblies to include the occasional memorials of popular saints, which in turn, through proliferation, led to daily Mass. And through the influence of the religious orders in the Middle Ages, courtly affectations, courtesies, and gestures of homage, such as genuflection, processions, and incensing of the sacrament, gave rise to cultic practices—and, in primitive societies, superstitions—that the Reformation would ridicule and try to halt.

Our church calendar was checkered with them: monthly Benediction, in which the Host was enshrined in a golden monstrance for what was once called "occular communion," and was used to solemnly bless the congregation at the conclusion of a liturgical service; the Forty Hours devotion, in which the Blessed Sacrament was venerated to commemorate the night and day of Christ's Passion; the yearly festival of Corpus Christi, a celebration of eucharistic piety, in which parishioners were urged to increase their active participation in a Latin liturgy they could only follow in the English translation of their *Saint Joseph Missal.* Monsignor Flanagan went still further by instituting at Holy Angels perpetual adoration: The church was open twenty-four hours a day, seven days a week, with one or two parishioners continuously there, praying before Christ in the tabernacle. There were many nights when, on a wander near the neighborhood, and in some state of crisis and desperation, I went inside the near-dark church for a "visit" and saw one or two adorers haloed by the glow of their reading lamps and silently kneeling on prie-dieux near the altar railing, generously giving up an hour of their day to say the rosary or page through their prayer books in a vigil that still strikes me as poignant and chivalrous.

In high school a Jesuit priest encouraged Rob and his classmates to go to weekly Confession, and so he went once, alone. As Rob was saying his prayers afterward, he scanned a church that was otherwise empty and stared at the veiled tabernacle where the Blessed Sacrament was kept, and he remembered the first line of Psalm 84, "How lovely is your dwelling place, O LORD of hosts!" Rob thought, *I have always been happy here*, and it was then he decided he would become a Jesuit.

I have never been so stunned as when he confided that to me.

The Jesuit vows of obedience, poverty, and chastity—particularly the latter—seemed hard, onerous, and positively scary to this high school boy. And I was cooling to the Church in my late teens and early twenties, not in the freefall-with-no-parachute way of so many Catholics who call themselves lapsed—I was still a weekly communicant—but oh what a scoffer I was, a lofty, incredulous, ever-objecting wiseguy slouching in the farthest back pew and just waiting for the priest to screw up. Which he often did in those years when the secrecy and panoply and weird accretions of the Tridentine Rite were giving way to the homely vernacular and folk guitar and roll-your-own liturgies. And the boredom, the abominable boredom. There were priests then—there regrettably still are—who seemed not to have read a theology book since their ordination, whose interest in their congregations seemed nil, whose homilies were dull, turgid, or haranguing, and who, were they professors offering elective classes in a university setting, would find themselves utterly without students.

I am talking about the sixties and seventies now, when rebellion was à la mode, but my crime was insubordination, not revolution, for I discovered that when I did not go to Mass I missed it. I felt serenity there, even joy, it seemed to make things good and right; and as my attendance at Mass increased in frequency, my sense of the rhythm, history, and logic of the liturgy also grew. Weather, busyness, and the doldrums could still hold me at bay, but for the most part I was hooked. A daily.

Often now when I find myself in a city of strangers, I find a local Catholic Church and go to the first morning or noontime Mass. And in the familiar structure of the eucharistic rites and the faith I presumably share with the assembly, I have a feeling of commonality, of long-lost family, of home.

Even in my childhood, most Catholics did not think it odd that the commemorative meal that the first Christians shared had changed through the ages into an object of adoration and reservation, nor that the simple dining rooms of the first centuries had given way to sanctuaries that resembled the holy of holies where the ark of the covenant was kept. The laity were little more than an afterthought in the rubrics of the *Roman Missal*, and their noninvolvement made it easy to ignore what was going on: It was not uncommon at Mass to see a parishioner strolling around the church lighting votive candles, oblivious to the Consecration even as the shaken bells heralded it. We were called members of Christ's Mystical Body, the Church, but our participation in liturgies was limited to serving the priest, ushering, singing in the choir. We, the unordained, could not touch the consecrated bread, nor the ciborium that contained it. We did not drink the wine. Women could not go beyond the altar railing except for chores like cleaning and lily arranging.

I recall one morning when I was serving the assistant pastor at Communion, holding the gold-plated paten under the chins of those who were receiving so the Host would land on the paten and not the floor should the wafer slip from their tongues. Monsignor

Flanagan was helping out by giving Communion farther down the railing, and I heard him roar, "Don't you *dare* touch that!" With shock I turned to see Monsignor in one of his hot-tempered rages, screaming chastisements at a cringing old woman who'd had the gall to try retrieve a fallen Host. *With her hands.*

Rules were rules, after all.

But the Second Vatican Council changed them. In order to regain the spirit of the Gospels and the liturgical celebrations of the first Christians, Vatican II urged the conscious and active participation of the laity in the Eucharist. Rescinding the prohibition against vernacular languages in the Roman rite, increasing the number and content of biblical readings, reestablishing old customs such as Communion in the hand and of both kinds, permitting the laity to act as deacons, lectors, psalmists, and ministers of the Eucharist, Vatican II sought an *aggiornamento*, a renewal or updating of the institutes and practice of the Church. And it accomplished its goal as no council had since Trent.

I was a lector at Mass for many years before I became a eucharistic minister. I was a college professor, after all, and had read my own fiction in public hundreds of times, so it was not particularly daunting to stand at the lectern, or ambo, and read aloud the Hebrew scriptures, the responsorial psalm, the epistle. Words were familiar and safe. To hand Christ's body and blood to the congregation at Mass, however, seemed such a staggering and godly thing to do that I felt too unworthy to try it.

Then I realized there was an important theological point in that: I am, as we all are, a sinner; but in Christ I am as loved and forgiven as the good thief on the cross; in him my faith and worthiness are sufficient.

And so at noon Mass in the old California mission church of Santa Clara, I have the courage to go up to the tabernacle, genuflect before it just as Monsignor Flanagan would, and get out a ciborium I would not have dared touch in my childhood. And I stand where a railing used to be, holding the consecrated elements of either bread or wine, giving Christ to those holier than me, who walk up with such reverence, simplicity, seriousness, and childlike vulnerability that my eyes sometimes film with tears. It is a gift to me, that giving; it's the glorious feeling I have when I am writing as well as I can, when I feel I am, in ways I have no control of, an instrument of the Holy Being; for I have just an inkling of what Jesus felt when he looked on his friends in mercy and aching love, and I have a sense of why, just before he died, he established this gracious sacrament of himself.

Works Cited

Achtemeier, Paul J., ed. *Harper's Bible Dictionary.* San Francisco: Harper & Row, 1985.

Carroll, James. *An American Requiem: God, My Father and The War that Came Between Us.* Boston: Houghton Mifflin, 1996.

Catechism of the Catholic Church. New York: Doubleday, 1995.

Chesterton, G. K. "Heretics." Vol. 1 in *The Collected Works of G. K. Chesterton,* ed. David Dooley. San Francisco: Ignatius Press, 1986.

Coles, Robert. *The Call of Stories: Teaching and the Moral Imagination.* Boston: Houghton Mifflin, 1989.

Dalmases, Candido de. *Ignatius of Loyola, Founder of the Jesuits: His Life and Work.* St. Louis: The Institute of Jesuit Sources, 1985.

Dinesen, Isak. "The Supper at Elsinore." *Seven Gothic Tales.* New York: Vintage Books, 1972

———. "Babette's Feast." *Anecdotes of Destiny.* New York: Vintage Books 1993.

Doggett, Martha. *Death Foretold: The Jesuit Martyrs in El Salvador.* Washington, D.C.: Georgetown University Press, 1993.

Dudon, Paul. *St. Ignatius of Loyola.* Milwaukee: The Bruce Publishing Co., 1949.

Eliot, T. S. *Selected Essays.* New York: Harcourt, Brace & World, 1969.

Emminghaus, Johannes H. *The Eucharist: Essence, Form, Celebration.* Collegeville, Minn.: The Liturgical Press, 1981.

Fitzgerald, F. Scott. *The Last Tycoon.* New York: Charles Scribner's Sons, 1941.

Fitzgerald, George. *Handbook of the Mass.* New York: Paulist Press, 1982.

Flanagan, P. A. *It Is the Mass That Matters.* Omaha: By the author, Holy Angels Church, 1956.

Ford, Richard. "Reading." *Antaeus* 59 (Autumn 1987): 39–51.

Forster, E. M. *Aspects of the Novel.* New York: Harcourt Brace, 1985.

Ganss, George E. *The Spiritual Exercises of Saint Ignatius.* Chicago: Loyola University Press, 1992.

Gardner, John. *The Art of Fiction.* New York: Alfred A. Knopf, 1984.

________. *On Writers and Writing.* Reading, Mass.: Addison-Wesley, 1994.

Garnett, Edward, ed. *Conrad's Prefaces to His Works.* New York: Haskell House Publishers, 1971.

Godwin, Gail. "What's Really Going On." *Antaeus* 59 (Autumn 1987): 110–114

Gonçalves da Cãmara, Luis. *The Autobiography of St. Ignatius Loyola.* New York: Harper & Row, 1974.

Green, Thomas H. *When the Well Runs Dry: Prayer Beyond the Beginnings*. Notre Dame, Inkd.: Ave Maria Press, 1979.

Holmes, Urban T. *A History of Christian Spirituality.* San Francisco: Harper & Row, 1980.

Komonchak, Joseph A., Mary Collins, and Dermot A. Lane, eds. *The New Dictionary of Theology.* Wilmington: Michael Glazier, 1988.

LaVerdiere, Eugene. *Dining in the Kingdom of God.* Chicago: Liturgy Training Publications, 1994.

Lucas, Thomas M. *Saint, Site, and Sacred Strategy: Ignatius, Rome, and Jesuit Urbanism.* Rome: Biblioteca Apostolica Vaticana, 1990.

McDermott, Alice. "Confessions of a Reluctant Catholic." *Commonweal,* February 11, 2000.

Mackenzie, Norman H. *A Reader's Guide to Gerard Manley Hopkins.* Ithaca: Cornell University Press, 1981.

________. *The Poetical Works of Gerard Manley Hopkins.* Oxford: Oxford University Press, 1990.

Martin, Robert Bernard. *Gerard Manley Hopkins: A Very Private Life.* New York: G. P. Putnam's Sons, 1991.

Meissner, W. W. *Ignatius of Loyola: The Psychology of a Saint.* New Haven: Yale University Press, 1992.

Mitchell, Nathan. *Cult and Controversy: The Worship of the Eucharist Outside the Mass. Collegeville,* Minn.: The Liturgical Press, 1990.

Mulligan, Joseph E. "The Blood of Martyrs: The Seed of Hope and Commitment." *America,* February 17, 1990.

O'Connor, Flannery. *Mystery and Manners.* Edited by Robert and Sally Fitzgerald. New York: Farrar, Straus and Giroux, 1981.

O'Malley, John W. *The First Jesuits.* Cambridge, Mass.: Harvard University Press, 1993.

Ong, Walter J. *Hopkins, the Self, and God.* Toronto: University of Toronto Press, 1986.

Phillips, Catherine, ed. *Gerard Manley Hopkins.* Oxford: Oxford University Press, 1986.

Rahner, Hugo. *Ignatius the Theologian.* New York: Herder and Herder, 1968.

_______. *The Vision of St. Ignatius in the Chapel of La Storta.* Rome: Centrum Ignatianum Spiritualitatis, 1979.

St. Albans, Suzanne. *Magic of a Mystic: Stories of Padre Pio.* New York: Clarkson N. Potter, 1983.

Smolarski, Dennis C. *Eucharistia: A Study of the Eucharistic Prayer.* New York: Paulist Press, 1982.

Sobrino, Jon. *Companions of Jesus: The Jesuit Martyrs of El Salvador.* Maryknoll, N.Y.: Orbis Books, 1988.

Stone, Robert. "The Reason for Stories: Toward a Moral Fiction." *Harper's Magazine* 276 (June 1988).

Thomas, Alfred. *Hopkins the Jesuit.* London: Oxford University Press, 1969.

Updike, John. *More Matter.* New York: Alfred A. Knopf, 1999.

Weil, Simone. *Waiting for God.* New York: Harper & Row, 1973.

Whitfield, Teresa. *Paying the Price: Ignacio Ellacuría and the Murdered Jesuits of El Salvador.* Philadelphia: Temple University Press, 1994.

Wilson, Ian. *Stigmata.* San Francisco: Harper & Row, 1989.

COPYRIGHT ACKNOWLEDGMENTS

Grateful acknowledgment is made to the following, for permission to reprint previously published material.

"Writing as Sacrament," *Image: The Journal of Religion and the Arts*, Spring 1994.

"Faith and Fiction," *America*, April 1998.

"What Stories Are and Why We Read Them," *The Writer's Chronicle*, May 2000.

"A Nineteenth-Century Man," *Story*, Summer 1992.

"The Wizard: Remembering John Gardner," *New Myths/MSS*, II:2/III:1, 1995.

"The Pilgrim: Saint Ignatius of Loyola," *A Tremor of Bliss: Contemporary Writers on the Saints*, Paul Elie, editor, Harcourt Brace, 1994.

"The Story of Cain," *Genesis: As It Is Written*, David Rosenberg, editor, HarperCollins, 1996.

"Affliction and Grace: Religious Experience in the Poetry of Gerard Manley Hopkins," *Ministry*, Volume 1, May 1993. Introduction to the essay published as "Hopkins and I" in *The Hopkins Quarterly*, Spring 1999.

"Leo Tolstoy's 'Master and Man,'" *You've Got to Read This*, Ron Hansen and Jim Shepard, editors, HarperCollins, 1994.

"*Babette's Feast*," *Writers on Film: 27 Writers Celebrate 27 Memorable Movies*, Jim Shepard, editor, HarperCollins, Fall 2000.

"*Anima Christi*," *Hosanna*, February/March 1993.

"Stigmata," *Things in Heaven and Earth*, Harold Fickett, editor, Paraclete Press, 1998.

"Hearing the Cry of the Poor: The Jesuit Martyrs of El Salvador," *Martyrs*, Susan Bergman, editor, Harper San Francisco, 1996.

"Eucharist," *Signatures of Grace*, Tom Grady and Paula Huston, editors, E.P. Dutton Publishers, 2000. Excerpted as "My Daily Bread," *America*, March 18, 2000.